Alcoholism and Addiction –

A Secular Ten-Step Program

By Robert Villegas

Alcoholism and Addiction – A Secular Ten-Step Program
By
Robert Villegas

Contact: robertv1989@outlook.com

ISBN-13: 978-1539315346

Published in the United States of America

Series Title: Villegas Self-Improvement Volume 2

www.robertvillegas.com

Dedicated to My Father

Robert Regino

Table of Contents

Introduction

> "Is it the gods who...put in our hearts / This burning desire...or else / Does each man make of his own wild yearning a god?"
>
> - Virgil, The Aeneid

The ideas in this book provide a secular approach to addiction that is founded on real values that the individual identifies for himself. This departs from the traditional religious views that impose altruism as a prime value. According to the traditional view, your prime value should be other people and serving them – it should not be about you. I wrote this book to help develop a new model for people trapped in the cycle of addiction. It is my view that the religious premises of the current Alcoholics Anonymous organization must be re-considered. As I made my journey through substance abuse, I had the opportunity to observe these premises and I judged them as defective because they didn't relate to my life and circumstances. As a consequence, I had to develop a different path that worked for me.

The ideas, and especially the ten-step secular program offered in this book, are based upon my own battle with addiction. I want to state clearly that I am not a professional working in the field of addiction; I am an individual who has dealt with addiction as part of my own private struggle. I do not hold myself out to be a counselor, a psychologist, psychiatrist or a doctor of any kind specializing in the field. I am a person who dealt with these issues as part of my own private struggle. What I learned about myself and the issue of addiction is based upon my own experiences. I had to develop my own knowledge, my own intellectual tools and I do not hold these ideas out to be the final answer that will create a life-changing metamorphosis for my readers. I hope they help but I make no guarantees.

I offer these suggestions for your consideration as well as for the consideration of counselors who are seeking new tools and a new understanding of addiction that does not provide the obligatory religious perspective. In fact, my perspective is secular – without religion – and I think this perspective might provide some interesting insights for counselors mired in the repetition of old and unworkable faith-based ideas that have provided little in the way of understanding in the past. My approach is secular but also "cognitive". I focus on knowledge and the process needed for "changing one's mind" rather than for merely changing one's actions. I offer no miracles and no promises. I am merely suggesting that the key to addiction, as I have learned, is found in reason, the mind and changing what one thinks.

To put it bluntly, the religious approach to addiction is counter-productive and even harmful. Certainly, the advocates of the religious approach want to help alcoholics and their dedication and hard work should be appreciated. However, I think there is a better secular way. It is hoped that this approach will assist the reader in also beginning his own journey of understanding.

Part 1. Setting the Foundation

Theoretical Framework

Alan is the son of an alcoholic. His father drinks repeatedly and the family is in constant turmoil. Either he can't sleep because of his father's tirades or he worries about his mother being harmed by his anger. He hears him screaming late at night to his mother and fears his becoming violent. Sometimes he is angry and tries to confront the father while at other times he remains silent fearing even more violence.

He listens to the loud noises while he lies silent in his room under the cover of a blanket, as his father drones on about his right to enjoy life and do as he pleases. He listens as his father accuses his wife and family of trying to restrict his freedom. These arguments go on for hours, night after night and he feels his father's anger at an oppressive family of religious freaks. The confusion, the doubts and the fears he feels are experienced as a huge package full of terrible ideas and he wonders if he is really the criminal in this family. He does not know what to do or what to think.

Later, as an adult, he finds little peace and tremendous self-doubt. Now away from the cruelties of his father's late-night rants, he is still unable to sleep because of his nightmares and he wonders what is wrong with his life. Because he is confused, he refuses to marry and occasionally he has a drink to help drown the doubt, but even this gives him a false sense of "normalcy". He finds himself rationalizing his desire to drink by resurrecting his father's old arguments and taking on a confrontational attitude toward an overly-moralistic "society". Slowly, over time, he does not notice that he has become his father. The only thing he knows is that after a few drinks, he feels better, freer, more friendly and less confused.

Jessica has a similar childhood except her parents are not alcoholics or enablers. They are television junkies. Her father was an unemployed grocery store clerk who couldn't seem to rise above that role. He worked many jobs until finally he was laid off by a grocery store chain that was closing stores in his region. He spent most of his time on unemployment, welfare and with his food stamps managed to feed his family.

Eventually, he got comfortable with this situation and decided on a scheme to stay on the dole. He got a job at another grocery store chain and faked an accident that left him "immobile" and unable to work. He began drawing disability payments and continued to spend his time on the couch and/or working around the house. The family was not able to get much in the way of nourishing food and Jessica came to enjoy the time in front of the TV set watching daytime game shows and soap operas. She became so captivated by these shows that she and her father spent most of their days snacking and watching television.

Jessica became addicted to the pleasure of the sedentary life where she enjoyed exotic tastes in snacks and hours of television time. As she grew, people noticed that she was a little chubby and that she seldom played outside and did much in the way of physical activity. They didn't take much notice until after she was married and continued her lifestyle –

while her husband was away working in a factory. At this point, she blew up like a balloon and started telling people that her whole family was made up of "big-boned" people and there was nothing she could do about it. She continued to spend her daytime in front of the television set and her nighttime as well since her husband seemed to always excuse himself to get out at night and visit the bars with his friends, play pool and otherwise enjoy his time off of work.

By the time Jessica was 30 years old, she weighed 300 pounds and by 35, 400 pounds. She had become addicted to television and pleasure foods. Her husband left her, she went on welfare because she couldn't work and her children also began to go out as often as possible to avoid her.

Susie was a hard-working mother. As a divorcee, she had learned how to make it on her own. She worked in a transportation company call center and earned a good salary because of her pleasant voice and intelligence. When she broke her leg in an unfortunate auto accident, everyone knew that she would heal quickly and get back on her feet. The doctor gave her some medicine to deal with her pain and she learned that the pills gave her a pleasant "high". It seemed to smooth over some of what she called her "rough edges". After her leg healed and there was no need for medicine, she began to wonder how she might get some medicine to help her out from time to time. She found friends who were on pain medications and sometimes she borrowed a few pills. Then she decided to see if she could get a doctor to prescribe some pills so she told her doctor her broken leg was still hurting to see if she could get them. She constantly told her doctors about her leg pains; headaches; psychological problems and, over time, she was getting several different medications from several different doctors; most of whom did not know what the other doctors were prescribing. Her boss started asking her about her inconsistent work and pointed out that her production and quality had been falling so she filed a grievance against her boss for harassment. Needless to say, her boss was perplexed and felt helpless when it came to trying to improve her production.

Eventually, the situation exploded when she tried to move her office chair and fell onto the floor and collapsed into unconsciousness. Later, in the hospital, she had to admit the various medications she was taking and the doctor informed her that what she was getting from one doctor was in conflict with the medication she was getting from another. So much for smoothing out the rough edges. She was now a full blown drug addict and was ordered by her employer to get treatment or lose her job. After several months of counselling and grievance filing, she fell out of her chair again and lost her job.

One night while 11-year old Johnny turned over in his bed, he accidentally brushed his arm against his penis and felt a tinge of pleasure in that area. It felt so good that he touched himself again and again and found even more pleasure. He continued to do this until something unexpected happened. He had an intense release and ejaculated a strange liquid onto his mattress. Not only was this strange and exciting to him but it was also fearful. What was wrong with his body and why did it feel so good?

He knew that this pleasure was something he wanted to experience again. Yet, he was afraid to ask anyone about it because his parents had warned him against doing wicked things that offended God. This must surely be one of them, he thought. He did some Google searches and tried to find out what was happening to him and found an article that explained it but his parents had blocked the content from his computer. So he went to the public library after school the next day to see what he could learn.

He found out that what he was doing was called "masturbation" and that it was a normal bodily process that he should enjoy without guilt. He was buoyed by this discovery and decided to learn as much as possible about his sexual nature and use his new knowledge to achieve happiness. A new world opened up to him because he also learned that men and women could experience sexual pleasure together and significantly enhance their enjoyment as lovers. He goes home happy about future prospects. What happened to him was normal and he looked forward to integrating his new knowledge of sex into his life.

But when he gets home, he is confronted by his mother who has discovered the stains on his bed sheets. Too embarrassed to speak, he holds his head down and listens to her drone on about the devil and how it uses pleasure to lead us astray and how he should fight temptation and forsake sex altogether. She tells him not to masturbate anymore and to seek God's forgiveness in the confessional.

When he goes to Church, he confesses his sin to the priest who asks him very personal questions; how long has he been doing this? What other things is he thinking about and does he feel impure? He answers haltingly and the priest suggests that they have a private consultation and asks him to come to his quarters later that day.

Too embarrassed to continue, he does not keep the appointment with the priest and wonders what all the fuss is about and why other people are trying to influence his private thoughts and newly discovered pleasures. He decides never to talk to anyone about it again and to do everything he can to get back to a normal life without masturbation.

He tries to force himself to stop masturbating but the pleasure is so powerful that he gives into it. For some reason, he cannot force his body to stop the desires so he does everything possible not to feel them. He is caught in a trap.

By trying to fight off the needs of his body for pleasure he sets up a personality split which consists of a war between what his mind (and the spirit) wants which is purity without sex and what his body wants which is to enjoy pleasure. The result is suppression of pleasure and an inner struggle that leaves him constantly fighting himself.

———————

These are just a few examples of people who use "pleasure" to escape their problems. What are the characteristics of these forms of addiction?

- People have problems in life usually childhood trauma
- Many of these problems involve conflict with others

- In order to feel better, they find something that is socially acceptable but take it to extremes
- They tell themselves to lie to themselves about what they are doing which enables rationalization of their actions
- They have a distorted value hierarchy where a particular pleasure is more important than all the values they possess – but they never acknowledge that this value conflict is a problem – they block the contradiction from their minds

The hallmark of the addict is an inability to use reason at critical decision points in his or her life. In order to have a proper morality, the individual must have an effective connection to reality. He must be able to project those values through a series of actions that result in successful living. His values must be consciously chosen by a process of reason and there must be no subconscious baggage.

When his only thought is to ameliorate physical or psychological pain, the only respite is found in physical pleasure. For this individual, pleasure eliminates (or blocks) pain and becomes the only value in life. This creates an exaggerated sense of pleasure and makes it the solution to painful living, self-doubt, confusion, anxiety and fear of others. This causes addiction and poor living choices.

To make this clear, let's imagine the case of an overweight person. This individual has become overweight because he lost the connection between how to have a healthy body and his desire to be healthy. Since this individual has little self-esteem, there is little motivation that would spur the action that would enable health, vigor and a toned body.

Deciding to count calories, going to the gym and exercising do not require rocket science, yet this person would prefer to live in a cocoon of fantasy, where he can avoid various activities, people and interests and replace them with eating. The result is a decline in health, exercise and appearance. In order to ameliorate pain and anxiety, the individual "avoids" life in favor of pleasure choices (food in this case) and this distorts his life.

Likewise, the sexually addicted person prefers

to function in a sexually-charged fantasy world of his own making. Somewhere deep in this person's psyche, there is a desire to please people. This destroys his ability to discriminate between people of value and no value. It turns him into a sexual altruist who obtains his own pleasure by giving it to others.

Sex (and having sex) is the easiest way for a troubled individual to get approval because during sex, most often, there is only approval. Also, the sexual relationship enables the person to re-enact and reverse painful trauma from early life. The sex addict cannot bring to his sexual decision-making a valid way of deciding with whom to have sex. This person drifts in a sexual fog of unrealized thoughts, pleasing all and loving all because he was taught that everyone is better than he.

Because the approval of others is thought necessary for survival by so many, it can become the basis for addiction. The drive for approval must be pursued at all times and in all ways. In this state, he develops a one-track mind with all choices based upon, not self-interest and logic, but upon gaining approval.

Likewise, the troubled individual discovers that when he is high on drugs or alcohol that it is easier for him to be more affable, friendlier and free. You could almost say that these good feelings help him connect to others more easily and make him feel that he is a better person when he is high. Without the drug, he feels stale, restricted, unhappy and unspontaneous. With the drug, he is a "man about town", happy and self-confident.

For the person disconnected from reality, promiscuous choices rule life, determine daily routines, career choices, life-partner choices and sexual preferences; these are all moral decisions. As if looking into a reversed mirror, this individual sees himself and his self-worth reflected back to him in the expressions on the faces of others, the moods of others, the nameless communications that may or may not be approval and may or may not be hatred at the same time. Addiction most often comes from the need to feel approval and the drive to do what it takes to get it. The need for approval is often the addiction within the addiction.

Whether the individual is a gigolo or an "easy

woman", the principle is the same; when the individual is taught to please others above oneself then the most profound expression is to please them sexually. Add sex to collectivism and you have promiscuity, the over-powering need to have sex with almost anyone. Then add guilt over sexual promiscuity and you have an automaton that never learns to enjoy life while pursuing only pleasure.

The addicted individual, because this thinking is disconnected from reality, loses the ability to connect new knowledge to life's problems. This is why I call him "disconnected". By rationalizing his actions to himself, so to speak, he becomes consumed with making words appear to fit reality rather than fit his understanding to reality. For instance, the religious person looks at words in sacred texts and attempts to find meaning in life by interpreting the words as wisdom about life and morality. This approach reverses the relationship between reality and the mind and intervenes in the process of gaining knowledge. In effect, he asserts that knowledge is "ready-made" and given by God, fed directly into his mind. The result is the spectacle of some men imposing their views on other men who must base their lives upon it.

Religion is not without a role in creating addiction – in spite of its protestations against immorality. Religion is based upon the idea that one can reason from unsupported moral ideas that derive from a deity. This thought process is called rationalism. Rationalism is a subconscious acceptance of false unverifiable knowledge. When the individual receives messages that tell him he is evil, that man is doomed and that he should spend his life sacrificing for others, the conflict is between knowledge that doesn't work and real knowledge which sets the individual reeling psychologically. The individual then becomes addicted to the fantastical, the miracle, the unproven and unfounded. Reality means nothing and floating abstractions mean everything. When God commands man to be altruistic, according to religious leaders, there is no mind to question it, no reference in reality, no thought that there might be something wrong with this command.

Addiction, psychologically, begins with this

conflict between rationalism and objectivism.

The pressure of having to endure disapproval and denigration from others based upon false charges, justified by rationalistic messages, creates a crisis of self-confidence within the individual that develops into the "knowledge" that he is inferior and fated to be in conflict with others. Psychological pain is the result. It is this conflict that religion brings into the AA 12-Step program that we will discuss later.

When an addict takes a self-destructive course, it is because of the logic of his subconscious knowledge. Actions based upon this kind of "knowledge" destroy appropriate action and the possibility of morality and action. This impels the addict to pursue the pleasurable self-destructive act that makes him feel better and releases him to act in an amoral way. The drive toward amorality feels like an imperative because it is coming from a subconscious need to be free to act, to feel better and to live normally. The conclusion the individual draws is that the addictive behavior is so pleasurable or fulfills such a positive need that it is more important than all other things he does. It is a form of rebellion against religious or moral imperatives.

When the pursuit of moral action is restricted through the fear of others, it is the ego and even the need for pleasure that must be controlled. Cynics, who understand that man cannot control the urges toward pleasure, are quick to take advantage and offer pleasure in seedy, guilt-producing fashion through sex clubs, pornography, alcoholic beverages, drugs, and other demeaning temptations — and they make millions of dollars in the process.

The individual, with a need to escape the pain and anxiety, can only pursue his pleasures out of sight, protected from the eyes of those that would judge him to be evil. This is why many bars and clubs, even sex clubs, are dark and shrouded in secrecy – they are the forbidden (by religion) and must be done out of sight. To this extent, religious morality creates the very acts it forbids and sends man into guilt and depression because, after all, god is watching. That there is nothing for which to feel guilty does not occur to the poor addicts who crave normalcy in a world of cynical forbidden pleasures; a world where self-esteem is destroyed by the low esteem society places on the individual.

The more the individual fears doing what he wants, the more he feels subconsciously that he needs to be free. Addiction becomes a solution that most assuredly works to release the core, the inner self and the suppressed ego. Addiction helps him forget that he is afraid of the opinions of others. But since it is a blind release into mindlessness, it is also destructive because there is no moral base to counter irrational acts. What was undertaken for pleasure and release becomes a problem of inappropriate and self-destructive action.

There are many periods throughout history when sexual expression was considered evil. The result was that "good" people who tried to repress their sexual nature actually intensified it and made it unavoidable. During the middle ages, these behaviors were often thought to be caused by the devil, but the real devil was the Church's belief that sexual pleasure was sinful. During many periods, the Church burned these people as witches and demons regardless of whether they were guilty of anything. The mere hint or suspicion of self-directed action was a proof that the devil was involved. The Church no longer burns witches and heretics – it just kills them intellectually.

Guilt feelings from inappropriate behavior create a crisis of motivation and self-doubt that moves the individual to more intensely control the inexorable movement toward pleasure. But because of the persistent nature of the anxiety, the pursuit of pleasure takes a "life of its own" and makes the individual feel that there is something bad or immoral about him, creating moral dualism, yin yang, a constant struggle of "good vs. evil" within the individual – within this struggle, normal pleasure and the mind are linked to evil – the perfect trap to keep the individual "believing".

Eventually, the individual's efforts to control addiction (his drive for pleasure) create a perpetual cycle, a sort of roller coaster ride, of denial and acceptance which leads to increasing tension that eventually threatens the health of the body through real and psychosomatic illnesses. This conflict is characterized by anxiety, the fear of being discovered as an innately evil person.

Notice that the culprit and the beneficiary of addiction is religion. Addiction is always associated with pleasure and, according to religion, pleasure is always associated with guilt. I call religion's view hatred of the ego – and it creates a vicious cycle that goes back to the mystery religions and their methods. The mystery religions were more honest in recognizing that their teachings created fear and they sought, through their rituals, to countenance orgiastic release as part of ritual catharsis.

In fact, addiction, ritual and fantasy are synonymous in that they are each a method of releasing emotional and sexual tension. The role of fantasy, the mystery rites, early forms of drama and ritual re-enactments have barely been investigated in our culture, yet they can all be methods of avoiding fear of hatred from society and culture. They are, in essence, forms of addiction.

When the addicted individual "learns" that a particular activity is doing harm to him (and since his wellbeing is not important (sacrifice is)), he learns not to put himself at the center of his moral choices. This forces him to disregard his own wellbeing and put others at the center of his concerns. This creates a conflict regarding his own real and now anxious behaviors. So he feels compelled to please others even more intensely and this creates even more anxiety which needs release by means of cathartic pleasure.

Reason cannot penetrate this fantasy/altruism cocoon because of the "protections" the individual has set up to keep himself from recognizing his addiction. When he is not being "sinful" through his addiction, he is being altruistic and using the illusion of "goodness" to counter it. He begins to think of himself as a phony pretending to be good. But when the impulse to enjoy the addiction takes hold, he begins a process of telling his mind to convince himself that his desire for his addiction is actually a positive justifying motive.

Even under the influence of his addiction, his paramount thought is still of others, what they think, how they would react, how he can affect or manipulate them and how to rationalize his behavior to them. Outside of his addiction, others are still the center of his thoughts because they (family or society) disapprove of his behavior and demand self-sacrifice. He is sent between having a rebellious nature that demands pleasure and a guilty nature that demands he revoke pleasure.

The addict always pretends to be a normal person. Many addicts rationalize their addiction as a "normal" pursuit of pleasure. These rationalizations make addiction difficult to overcome because they "seem" to justify addictive behaviors. An addict can make himself seem like a totally normal person but one thing is true: his only concern in life is feeling better because he feels so bad. If he can manage to somehow survive, so much the better. In fact, many addicts pursue success in business in order to be able to afford their addictions.

The role of fantasy is important for the addict. Fantasy creates a separate reality for the person who is racked by pain. Fantasy is an escape that creates a different form of living; a cocoon of pleasure. Fantasy is addiction, it is what happens when the individual is escaping; it is the benefit the addict seeks, it is the universe where the individual can do what he wants without fear of the opinions of others or the restrictions of religious morality. Fantasy is a make-believe world of freedom, a form of heaven.

Altruism and the guilt it induces is the most powerful force in the world. It forces moral decisions into the realm of crisis – when fear is most painfully experienced. What the individual learns in these crisis events is that the addiction, though full of freedom and released ego, contains an aftermath that is harmful or painful. He learns that the aftermath is more difficult to deal with than the addiction because it contains physical pain, embarrassment, legal problems and scarred relationships with loved ones and society, a lessening of moral status and even harm to those one loves.

The logical conclusion from this pain in crisis is that the addiction is harmful. Yet, even though the individual decides to no longer perform the addictive action (for as long as the pain is there) he loses the resolve he thought he had against it in a very short time. The power of the addiction as an anesthetic, the habit of avoidance it brings and the fearful, anxious emotions that caused the need for the anesthetic; all force the individual back into the addictive behavior and the fantasy cocoon that it makes possible. The individual begins once again to rationalize and self-authorize the addictive behavior – another cycle of the inner struggle begins.

The subconscious and single-minded goal that people seek when trying to resolve psychological problems involving addiction is the release of the ego – the freedom to act. But, because the individual does not get to the source of his pain, he is helpless against the attraction of the anesthetic. Addiction then is a harmful and artificial rebellion; an artificial form of freedom because the pleasure that comes from it anesthetizes fear and tensions and releases the normally suppressed ego. This is why an addict is so difficult to cure. **What appears to be a physical dependency in addiction is really a false psychological quest**

for a method of releasing suppressed ego.

From a broader perspective, collectivist, moralistic social institutions, and especially religion, are part of an elaborate scheme intended to suppress and control the ego of the individual. This is the essential perspective of the collectivist society's approach to addiction. Both mysticism and nominalism (skepticism) are essentially "attacks" on innocence, an effort to destroy the ego, reason and logical deliberation. They essentially put the individual in a prison made up of cultural, ethical, metaphysical and epistemological traps for the ego; they keep the ego from asserting its full rational nature.

The culturally trapped individual subconsciously rebels against this imprisonment and lashes out without having the intellectual tools to understand the enemy that keeps him imprisoned. The individual often accepts the validity of these cultural traps and, because mysticism and skepticism preach human intellectual incompetence, he never develops the tools that would help him escape from the prison of compliance and submission.

Addiction becomes his only alternative since it represents a quasi-rebellion against prevailing and oppressive norms.

How does an individual get to a point where destructive (addictive) action is so compelling that it is more important than constructive value-based action? I suggest that self-destructive action is based on fear of others and of their opinions. It is caused by the "cage" that the individual has been place within by social attack that deems him to be a sinful or imperfect being. Because religious premises are essentially based upon, not the word of a deity, but the opinions and pronouncements of other men, the individual learns to fear the negative opinions of others that are part of the religious or social experience. The anxiety felt by the individual severs the relationship between his mind and his judgment of reality and sends him on a course where anything that seems to alleviate anxiety and release paralysis is preferable to "normal" action. Addictive behaviors anesthetize the pain felt by the individual, and because these behaviors seem like valid solutions to the pain, they are preferable to being "a straight" person.

This morality vs. amorality split is the deadliest of all splits. It makes any morality that is different from altruistic morality into an evil idea and that includes self-love and rationally chosen values. The idea that morality is only represented by altruism is insidious because it only countenances self-sacrifice and denigrates the idea of self-concern, self-respect and self-interest. How can any person be healthy under the influence of altruism – altruism countenances hatred of self? How can any individual develop a strong enough sense of self to be able to counter the supposition that he is inferior, incompetent and evil by nature?

As a motivator of life, altruism can only lead to self-destruction of a kind that is angry, hateful and vicious. The answer to religion is not a-religion; the answer to theism is not atheism and the answer to morality is not amorality. The true answer is to find true morality through reason without the intervention of a spirit. We must go beyond religion and atheism if we are to solve the problem of addiction. We must deal with reality.

The AA 12-Step Program

A major part of the anti-man philosophy dominant today is reflected through the twelve-step program of the AA. Before we can learn about the flaws of this program, we must analyze the basic premises of each step. This will lead us to a better set of steps that can be followed. The following are the original twelve steps published by Alcoholics Anonymous:

- We admitted we were powerless over alcohol—that our lives had become unmanageable.
- Came to believe that a Power greater than ourselves could restore us to sanity.
- Made a decision to turn our will and our lives over to the care of God *as we understood Him.*
- Made a searching and fearless moral inventory of ourselves.
- Admitted to God, to ourselves, and to another human being the exact nature of our wrongs.
- Were entirely ready to have God remove all these defects of character.
- Humbly asked Him to remove our shortcomings.

- Made a list of all persons we had harmed, and became willing to **make amends to them all.**
- Made direct amends to such people wherever possible, except when to do so would injure them or others.
- Continued to take personal inventory, and when we were wrong, promptly admitted it.
- **Sought through prayer and meditation to improve our conscious contact** with God *as we understood Him,* praying only for knowledge of His will for us and the power to carry that out.
- Having had a spiritual awakening as the result of these steps, we tried to carry this message to alcoholics, and to practice these principles in all our affairs.

It is not my intention to attack religion. My goal is to help people caught up in addiction. To accomplish this, I must show how some religious concepts are harming that goal. So let's look at each step that the AA recommends:

We admitted we were powerless over alcohol — that our lives had become unmanageable.

This first step is essentially an admission of defeat. It admits that alcohol is such a powerful substance that once one becomes addicted one has no choice but to go down "the rabbit hole" so to speak. The only way out is to pay homage to the monster that rules the "under land" of alcoholism.

I submit that this gives too much credit to alcohol and ignores the power of the human mind and human values. When the culture is poised against creating rational values (i.e. values devised by the individual for his own self-interest), when it denigrates you for being "too selfish" or "too proud", it becomes your enemy, not your friend. When it uses unearned moral guilt against you – and more importantly, when you accept such guilt without fighting for your rational self-interest, what can you do but look for a way out of feeling guilty? That way out is often mistakenly going to lead you to seeking exaggerated pleasures rather than rational values.

In fact, it is not alcohol that man is powerless against; it is the cultural ideas that pass judgment over him that he can't control. They have trapped man in a state in which he has no power to change the negative assessments about his own power as a thinking individual. These powers insist that he establish a set of artificial controls over his life and actions (mostly his actions) and this restricts man to an artificial moral code that is oppressive and guilt-inducing. Men are "forced" by this morality to try to "control" themselves and this establishes a false motivation that can easily be overcome by the power of addictive pleasure.

By accepting the idea that you are powerless against alcohol, you also accept the commandment to restrict your rational pursuit of pleasure in positive ways. You must battle pleasure (as such) not just alcohol. This can only make matters worse and force you into a situation where you have no way out – except through addiction.

Came to believe that a Power greater than ourselves could restore us to sanity.

When moral choice becomes a matter of submitting to the will of God, what can morality be but self-denial? The critical question becomes denial of what? Denial of irrational pleasure; rational pleasure or both? When irrational feelings and rational desires are mixed into one package to be avoided, how is the individual to know proper action? How is he able to use his mind to decide when the combination of opposites is impossible for him to reconcile? Irrational feelings are considered superior to rational needs and desires because they are more immediate, more intense, more exciting while altruism, sacrificing for others, has no real immediate benefit. There has to be a better way.

Here we have to understand what I mean by the need for "a secular approach". I do not mean that you have to become an atheist or that you must engage in a crusade against God or religion. I am referring to the effort to keep religion out of your analysis of reality. A secular approach tries to look at reality first and rejects any approach that cannot be based upon reality such as mysticism (miracles), rationalism (floating abstractions) and two-dimensionalism (Platonism).

To give you an example of secularism, look at the provision in our Constitution about Congress not making any laws regarding religion. With this provision, the Constitution prohibited government from making any laws that favored or disfavored a religion. The result was a secular society in which religion was not only free of government interference but also could not interfere in governance. Secularism meant that in government religion was to be avoided as a factor.

If you live a secular life, you look for answers outside of religion so you can focus on reality. Needless to say, to take a secular approach would require some "anti-religious" views but the key is to begin the process of living in reality when it comes to the most important issues.

Likewise, a secular individual would recognize the freedom of all men to live without interference by religion (if they chose) but would also not allow that interference of religion in his own life. Certainly, this separation liberates religious morality but it also liberates "secular" morality or reality-based morality.

Why should you take a secular approach to addiction and seek reality rather than mysticism? I think this approach is the only approach that keeps the issue of addiction solely in your control and makes it possible for you to keep on topic rather than be diverted by the demands of religion. As we saw in the previous section, religious influences can contribute to the furtherance of addiction.

Made a decision to turn our will and our lives over to the care of God *as we understood Him.*

In other words, man is a weakling (morally) and can't do it on his own. He needs a miracle and this very fact belies morality.

Miracles, my friends, do not happen – this is a fact. There is no divine intervention; it is all based upon a belief that reality is subject to the will and intervention of a spirit. The secular approach removes this mysticism from a role in dealing with addiction. There is no evidence that using mysticism (or miracles) to solve problems of addiction has been effective in past cases. It also takes the individual away from a consideration of the thinking he must do in order to begin to understand his personal values and focus upon them.

In fact, mysticism creates a muddled approach to addiction. When you accept miracles, you accept a reality that is fluid and uncertain. This applies to your methods of thinking and can do much harm to you when it comes to understanding your addiction. If mysticism finds a cure for addiction, then must it not also be a cause of the kind of thinking that encourages you to avoid reality?

Made a searching and fearless moral inventory of ourselves.

This is a good step. In fact, this step alone overcomes all of the appeals to mysticism because it should require a rigorous process of knowing what one has done morally that has caused anxiety and a need to drown one's emotions in a sea of unconsciousness (pleasure). By understanding what you are doing inside your mind, you can get a better grip on what you can control. You can control your thinking about how you justify your actions and you can control your actions by understanding your own thoughts and emotions and how they relate to your pleasure choices.

But morality is not just about what you have done that is bad and admitting it. It is also about what you have done that is good. Too often, we are told to criticize our own actions, to admit to the harm we have done, to look for ways to please God. We are constantly told to love others but seldom are we told to love ourselves; to see the good in ourselves and to appreciate it.

Too often, the problem we encounter when we indulge in alcoholic beverages is that we are overwhelmed by bad judgments that we think we should make of ourselves and this often leads us to acting out anger at ourselves which puts us into a situation of needing relief, drinking too much. Seldom do we realize the good in ourselves, the good we have done, the people we have elevated and loved through our good actions. Seldom are we told about the moral actions we have taken – and this is clear with the 12-Step Program; it is a program of self-admonishment and joy can never be discovered by an over-emphasis on self-flagellation.

Admitted to God, to ourselves, and to another human being the exact nature of our wrongs.

This is essentially the acknowledgment of one's wrongs. I think this is important when it comes to anyone that we have harmed by our violation of moral propriety as well as in our conversations with ourselves regarding our "problems" but for the previous reasons stated, I'd prefer that we stay grounded in reality and reason rather than the ineffable. Admitting what we have done to hurt people and engaging in an effort of retribution are proper if the harm done is significant. Not all people have a relationship with God and this step more or less demands that one establish a relationship with an entity that cannot be proven to exist.

At the very least, it is important that one undertake a secular approach with an open attitude toward the idea that the answer to addiction need not lie with a deity but with the facts of reality. This establishes a focus that attempts to find truth and meaning by looking at what is real first and deriving everything one can from a universe where existence is, indeed, all that exists.

Were entirely ready to have God remove all these defects of character.

As I mentioned before, we are, with this step, asking for a miracle to be done by God. In other words, God is made into an active agent who heals addiction by the addict's act of believing in him. It is the idea that going over to God creates a change of mind and principle in the addict. Imagine telling someone that God's love or God's power cured your alcoholism; that a miracle of prayer made it possible for you to overcome your shortcomings. As wonderful as this sounds, it is not a powerful deterrent to addiction.

There is no connection intellectually between a decision to pray and a decision to stop addictive behavior. Indeed, it amounts to the hope of a miracle which very often keeps a person addicted. In fact, addiction is not prevented by such hope as there is no reason found in the act of praying that is directly related to addiction. A person can pray to be rid of the addiction but such prayer provides no argument against it. As wonderful as God is thought by many people to be, there is little likelihood that he has any desire or ability to help you with your singular problems. God, as many have come to know him, is simply too busy to pay attention to you.

Humbly asked Him to remove our shortcomings.

Once again, you are asking for a miracle which means you'll get nothing. It will all be in your mind and not in reality in spite of the fact that your addiction takes place in reality and in the choices you rationalize. Better to find mental tools that enable you to work with your mind to give you a chance to act on your own behalf rather than submit to a mystical entity or authority.

Made a list of all persons we had harmed, and became willing to make amends to them all.

This is good but isn't necessary now. What you need to do first is change your mind, change how you think and this will influence what you do and what you value. This step comports with the secular approach but you should be careful not to confuse it with an obligation or duty to serve others. Make amends in order to get yourself straight with your own needs not a demand that you sacrifice for others. Making up for the damage done to others through addiction is a proper goal. But, as I wrote above, work on yourself first, then make amends to whatever extent possible once you have secured your new life.

Made direct amends to such people wherever possible, except when to do so would injure them or others.

Once again, if you have done something to harm someone, then it is important to make amends and "pay the price" of your misdeeds. But, do so at the proper time. This practice is not essential to solving the riddle of why you engage in addictive behavior. Making amends is more important during the later process of "getting your life right".

Continued to take personal inventory, and when we were wrong, promptly admitted it.

Taking personal responsibility is not always about being wrong and admitting it. It is about putting your life in order and being successful. If you are constantly focusing on "when you were wrong" you should change your focus toward "getting right".

That comes first.

Sought through prayer and meditation to

improve our conscious contact with God *as we understood Him*, praying only for knowledge of His will for us and the power to carry that out.

Once again, we subordinate our own mind to the mind of a supposedly superior being. This lowers our own mental abilities and directs them toward the hope of a magical or more powerful mind that is able to bend reality to its will. According to this view, our only hope is to sync with the wishes of that reality under the false hope that doing so will bring us closer to knowing reality and be guided by a truer principle. This cannot work. What if there is no such mind and no such "truer" reality on that basis? Inevitably, one only gets the ideas of other men as a guide while those men proclaim themselves representatives of the gods and dictate to us our own thoughts. Your goal should be to understand yourself, your thoughts both conscious and subconscious in order to change what must be changed to gain true knowledge of yourself and what you are doing.

Having had a spiritual awakening as the result of these steps, we tried to carry this message to alcoholics, and to practice these principles in all our affairs.

Basically, this approach seeks to utilize the principle of "the evil eye" which, in this case enlists other people in the effort to stay off alcohol. This idea uses the basic concept of holding the individual in a perpetual state of being watched. Although the "buddy system" is not a bad concept to use in such cases, the key problem here is that it depends on just how good the buddy is at understanding the issues you have to deal with. If he is not good at articulating important issues regarding alcoholism, then his only value is to act as a moral authority without authority; which means as a disapproving guilt-dispenser.

What you need is not a spiritual awakening but a reality awakening. You need to come to grips with the very real facts that you must understand in order to advance your values and accomplish your better self.

The clear problem with the 12-step program is that it is mystically based and not focused on the individual and his value choices but on God and His values. This requires that the individual subordinate himself and his life to God rather than deal with his own real issues. *This makes the 12-point program into a recruitment tool for religion rather than an aid in solving issues of moral choice based upon real life.*

What you need is a change of mind *for you* not for God or others. You need to be clear about what you need in order to live a moral life. The secular approach means acknowledging that a moral life is possible for you. But the basis of this view of morality must be the real world not the ineffable supernatural world of religion. Man, especially confused man, does not need to be baffled by the miracle of God's redemption. He needs knowledge and clarity, a view of reality that can actually mean something that he can validate and understand. This is what I intend to bring forward in this book. My ten-step program will start with the real and end with the real.

How to Think

The key then for overcoming addiction is to help the individual learn how to question false admonishments and then reject them in favor of reason. This process is made harder by the fact that the individual has already built up a mechanism that supports the addictions he has chosen. As we will see, I call this process telling your mind to argue on behalf of the addictive behavior. By unraveling this process and changing the intellectual approach, the individual can get to the core of his psychology and begin the process of re-litigating the content of his mind. Once this new process becomes "automatized" emotionally, the individual will be able to re-build his life around rational choices.

This is not an easy process because culture countenances sacrifice of his mind rather than the rational use of it. This process of "guilting" is a major obstacle to rational deliberation because guilt countenances against self-interested action. So many individuals spend their lives apologizing for themselves to such a high degree that it is impossible for them to ever recover their sense of pride and self-interestedness.

This means that we must teach the individual how to interpret those false fears and how, eventually, to arrive at a state where he is no longer subconsciously under the control of fears; no longer living in the cage that leads to addiction. This requires a "re-balancing" of the individual by means of helping him re-organize his mind, cast off bad thinking, and develop a true relationship with reality. It requires a proper morality based in reason.

What is Knowledge?

This chapter is based upon the idea that knowledge is habit and that in order to change your habit of addiction, you must look at reality and change your knowledge.

When I first asked the question "what is knowledge?", I thought that knowledge was the acceptance and use of a scientifically developed fact. Yet I observed that what most people took as knowledge had been seldom developed scientifically but most often by trial and error within a very delimited context — in other words, this "knowledge" had been developed outside the realm of a systematic process of testing and comparing, reasoning and validation. Yet, it still functioned as knowledge.

Then I observed organized ritual practices that are common in religion (and society in general) and noticed that they are not based on knowledge but on faith. On the other hand, non-organized rituals, habits developed in living, are most often copied from the actions observed in our parents, peers and other authority figures. Some of these habits are indeed life-serving but the reasons for their acceptance is faith-based rather than rational.

What could this mean? Most of our actions, i. e. habits, are not reality-based. Why is this? We have been taught that "reasons" for action are not critical but instead are of secondary importance. This has to be a clue to the problem of addiction. How deeply engrained in us is the idea of doing things without a rational basis and does this give us a clue to the problem of harmful actions; the reasons for them?

Surprisingly, I found the answer in philosophy and the source was ancient Greece. Aristotle somehow knew what knowledge is and how it is practiced. And his definition sent me upon a quest that revealed to me the need for an entirely new paradigm in human psychology…and a recognition of the fundamental principles that give rise to knowledge and action based upon knowledge. While reading Aristotle, I read the following:

"Habit differs from disposition in being more lasting and more firmly established. The various kinds of knowledge and of virtue are habits, for knowledge, even when acquired only in a moderate degree, is, it is agreed, abiding in its character and difficult to displace..." –Categories

The first thing that occurred to me after reading this is that most psychological problems (including addictions) are "difficult to displace" and I wondered if mistakenly acquired knowledge is partly the cause of such problems. In fact, this quote answers a whole host of additional questions. For instance, "Why is knowledge a habit?"

A habit, according to Merriam-Webster, "…refers to an act repeated so often by an individual that it has become automatic with him." Surprisingly, one of the definitions Merriam and Webster gives for "habit" is disposition, which means that Aristotle must have meant that disposition is something automatic but not acquired. Knowledge then must be something acquired by means of thought or reason that yields, by the power of the understanding, a habitual action. Or as Aristotle seems to say, knowledge is habit.

So, according to Aristotle, it is the power of knowledge, the power of the certainty inherent in knowledge that gives it the power of habit and impels or motivates the individual to act according to the realities that knowledge puts forth.

The next question is "What is the opposite of habit?" and the answer is "ritual," something not based upon verified knowledge. The basic difference between habit and ritual is that the knowledge inherent in ritual seems to be lost.

This makes ritual into action that is unreasonable, un-scientific and dogmatic. Yet, ritual *is* action, and as we have seen, proper action must be based in habit that comes from valid knowledge.

Reality, in order to be understood, requires an affirmation, a statement of truth that creates knowledge and thereby habit. Ritual is created when the connection between the habit and the statement of truth is severed, while the succeeding generations continue to perform the act by rote. Ritual is misguided action because it is no longer connected to known knowledge. In fact, we cannot even devise believable circumstances or presumptions to determine what that lost knowledge is.

Ritual is associated with religion. It generally repeats and/or commemorates the actions of the gods and is therefore tied to religious morality and "the good" as defined by men who believe in the power of a religious entity. Yet, ritual, separated from its founding knowledge, cannot be superior to habit connected to valid knowledge. And this is the only difference between them. They are both based upon knowledge, but one type of action is copied and the other is developed by thought and evaluation.

True knowledge is acquired when people learn ideas and principles that can be applied to action. Habit is the automatic action that comes from knowledge. It can be appropriate action if the knowledge is based upon reason or inappropriate action if the knowledge is subjective or based upon rote memorization.
On the issue of the relevancy of knowledge, we must understand that knowledge is the key to correct action. If a person operates on questionable premises, he/she cannot possibly take appropriate action—and this is the key to understanding neurosis and other psychological problems.

In confronting emotions, it is important to recognize that the individual, in order to have a healthy mental state, requires a feeling of well-being or security. This includes an understanding of the implications of reality as it relates to his life and situation. The individual needs to be able to reason, to abstract from reality the true significance of any entity or event and its true implications rather than think from emotion. Knowledge, therefore, lies beneath nerve force and habit, and when relevant, it leads to appropriate action for the life of the individual. This is the foundation for the whole area of human psychology. Unreasoned or incorrect evaluations at an early age establish powerful avenues of relevancy, nerve force and habit and as a result, create the foundation for unhealthy thinking and habits. However, the fundamental issue is that man always acts on the foundation of knowledge (or presumed truth) and this fact means either that he acts on correct knowledge and benefits himself or upon incorrect knowledge and falters.

Likewise, if a person's reason for acting is to avoid perpetual discomfort and fear (through pleasure choices), his motive is disintegrated because what he "knows" (about pleasure) is incorrect – the tension (motivation) developed creates more discomfort over the long-term. On the other hand, if the reason for acting is long-term and survival-based through actual knowledge then the individual's motive is integrated and unnecessary action is eliminated. Pleasure becomes a value that is integrated with the broader context of a successful life and other higher values.

So how do you know that your habits are based upon knowledge rather than emotion? We've talked about understanding your values, not telling your mind to lie to you, arguing with yourself and the principle of anti-thesis. All of these devices can help you gain certainty. True knowledge is cognitive in nature; this means it helps you see reality as it is; and *this* is how you see reality.

It *is* all about you

The real issue, when it comes to dealing with your addiction, is not that you have a physical dependency on a particular addictive substance or activity. The real issue is that you need to learn how to think so you are not psychologically compelled to do things that are harmful for you. You need to learn that it IS all about you.

You are addicted because you are unhappy. You have been embarrassed by something in your life, you have no hope, you are alone, you are isolated and alienated in some way and this gives you pain. You take your substance (or activity) of choice because you want to feel better and in order to take it you must lie to yourself that your form of addiction is a normal desire for normal living. We're all familiar with the maxim "It is not about you" that is said often by preachers who want people to be more giving in the collection basket. The idea is a staple of altruism intended to minimize the individual. The assertion that "It is not about you" says that you are being selfish and that is a bad thing. You should change your behavior, according to this view, and all your actions should be about others rather than yourself.

I challenge this notion and I insist that it *is* all about you. It is all about your self-interest, your good, your life, your joys and values. It can *only* be about you. In order to beat your addiction, you must strive for your highest self and never compromise with anyone about your conviction that you are good. You must become the most inspired image of yourself.

But I am not writing here about a narcissistic sense of self-value. I'm talking about the fact that you have a responsibility to yourself to "know" what is good for you, to learn as best you can how you think so you can bring that good into your life, not for the sake of hurting others but for the sake of helping yourself. This has clear relevance to what you think about your addictions, how you enable them and how you justify them. It is all about you because it is you who is doing the wrong thinking that causes you to lose your self-interested values in favor of dis-values that happen to give you pleasure.

What does it mean to make your actions all about others? It means that your actions are not about you at all. But isn't it your actions that need to change? Aren't you the one who has messed up your life and don't you need your best mind in order to straighten out your life? If you aren't important, if it isn't about you, then what is it about?

Putting others first means they are more important than you and that you should dedicate your life to serving their needs. But what does that have to do with your stopping addictive behavior? Is the answer to addictive behavior that you owe others your service? Does it mean that by living for them you take your mind off the next drink? In fact, this dedication to others is nothing more than another form of addiction – a way to avoid pain.

Why aren't your bad choices about you? You make them, right? You decide to do them because you see some (although false) benefit in doing them. How does living for others cause you to lose the desire for addictive behaviors?

Self-sacrifice means that you give values up for others. That means your own values, for which you need the most attention, are irrelevant to you. Self-sacrifice means a loss to you of something that you value more than the people for whom you are giving them up (helping your loved one is usually not a sacrifice). Self-sacrifice is essentially mind-sacrifice; and this means that you must conform to the ideas of others first. Yet, your mind is (or should be) your highest value; the very value that you need in order to answer critical issues and solve your addiction.

I'm not talking about foregoing kindness, love and concern for others. I'm talking about something as basic as yourself – you are the only person who can be dedicated to solving your own issues – no one else. That means you have to think of yourself first. The last thing you want to sacrifice to others and their views is your mind. You need your mind, not only to survive, but also in order to solve your problems. Once you give up your mind to the ideas of others, you have given up your life.

Additionally, we are not speaking of being rebelliousness or having a general distrust of people. We are speaking of starting with your own mind and using it to the best of your ability. We are talking about independence, thinking with your own mind; learning what it takes to survive and making decisions that advance your life. Your difficulty with addiction is about *you*.

To understand why it is about you, we can look at this issue from an opposite perspective: why is it not about them? First of all, "they" are not connected to your body. They don't think for you but for themselves. Each of them is an individual and each has a different perspective and interests. None of them owe you your sense of self-respect, self-esteem or even love. They must take care of themselves and they have no obligation to take care of you. Those are facts. No one is responsible for taking care of you but you.

Few individuals know you well enough to be able to understand what you are going through with your addictive behavior. Only you have enough interest in this issue to learn what is going on inside you, why you do the things you do and how you can change yourself. It is not an easy task but it can't be made any easier by accepting the premises, views, ideas and opinions of people who do not have that much interest in you as an individual. Only you, as an individual, can change yourself and only you know (or can learn) what is going on inside of you and change it.

I don't think the cure for addiction is to connect better with people or to spend your time helping them in some way. I think the cure is for you to make the connection to positive values. The recovering addict learns that he must hold some principles in order to be successful and he convinces himself of the truth of those principles. The cure can only be affected by the desire to be happy, to experience values. It starts when you realize that you can't be happy if you destroy your values. The realization of this fact must become more powerful to you than the physical magnet that is addiction.

Changing your Mind

The key to understanding addiction is not only in finding the right answers to questions but in first asking the right questions that will yield the correct answers. Every question has a fundamental base and when we look at fundamental truths, we can learn the right questions.

Let's use a simple example first. The proposition, 2 + 2 = 4 can be considered usable because this "knowledge" is correct. You cannot find an instance where 2 + 2 equals a different sum. Now, we'll use a more complicated unit of knowledge. Let's assume that I observe several examples of people who have become drug addicts and I want to identify a general principle that explains this addiction. One would have to ask each individual (and each of them would have to tell the truth) why he chooses to engage in an action that harms him. The easy answer is that he is addicted; his body "needs" the action or substance so much that he has no ability to resist it. Or the individual could say he uses subconscious rationalizations to tell himself that his body needs the action or substance. In other words, his mind has chosen irrational value conflicts.

What if the truth is the second explanation and that many "addictions" are not really caused by an out-of-control body that can't help being drawn to a particular substance or activity?

I would like to suggest this second unit of knowledge is the true one. It can be tested and then used by people to help them deal with their addictions. This new theory is based upon the idea that the individual learns early in life that a specific form of pleasure seems to solve certain problems; it makes him feel better and more normal. The key is to identify the thinking that led to this conclusion and correct it. That is what this book is about.

If this theory is true, then addiction can be reversed by changing your mind; learning how your thinking contradicted your life-enhancing values and how you can bring your thinking back into line with them.

Before you can realize that you have a problem with alcohol or other addictive substances, you have to be able to analyze what you think and do. You have to become better at getting into your own head and recognize when you are providing yourself with false reasons for doing what you do. For instance, no one gets up in the morning and decides to give himself a hangover on purpose. You know about the pain of hangovers and yet you still get drunk. This is because you are giving yourself a "reason" to get drunk. What are those reasons?

- I deserve some pleasure
- I have to be sociable
- One or two drinks won't hurt me
- It is time to celebrate
- My wife drinks with me

- I've worked hard today
- I have money in my pocket
- I'm going out anyway, I might as well have a drink

All of these "reasons" ignore one important fact: you are going to get a hangover and most likely do something that will embarrass you, your wife or your friends. Why isn't that fact of a hangover or potential embarrassment enough to make you think twice about getting drunk?

Don't feel too bad about it; men have been making this mistake for millennia (as we'll see when we read about the world's first drunk). But it need not continue forever. There are ways to stop hurting yourself. There are ways to stop lying to yourself and create a positive force in your life. There are ways to be your better self.

Your Body does not Lie to you – It is Your Mind that Lies to You

I quarrel with the idea that addiction is solely a sickness of the body; that the body has learned to accept the presence of a poisonous (although pleasurable) substance or activity. I would like to argue for an entirely different cause of addiction. The body is not lying to you that a particular substance is needed; it is your mind that is lying to you and trying to convince you that the substance or activity is of value to your life.

Imagine the confusion in the mind of a person who is always lying to himself. How does this happen? The initial desire is to reverse cause and effect regarding moral worth. This individual feels wrong in some way and has chosen to deal with this feeling by invoking the *appearance* of moral worth rather than *earning* moral worth. This is a reversal of the role of moral worth in life. One does not obtain moral worth by trying to appear moral; one only gains it by being moral.

Needless to say, the effort to reverse morality is wrong. One should not attempt the "appearance" of virtues. One should attempt to actually *possess* them.

Many young people are heavily influenced by their alcohol-drinking fathers or mothers. According to most parents like this, they drink to relax and feel better. They routinely resist any effort by family and friends who want them to refrain. In fact, they vehemently complain that such efforts are a violation of their personal choices and integrity. Don't ask this parent to do what you want him to do. He or she would insist that he or she runs the family and no one has the authority to dictate what to do under any circumstance. It is his or her right to "relax".

All of this seems correct but with one small problem. When this person drinks, he is more argumentative and often comes home with bloody noses and black eyes. The people in his life are telling him that they don't like it when he drinks too much. It scares them and no one knows what will happen next. They hope that if he knows "this side" of his drinking (their feelings about it) he might realize that it is not such a good thing for him and for them.

What it means is that his mind is giving him all the "reasons" he needs in order to drink and at the same time he knows that he is lying to himself. The fact the he doesn't care that it hurts and causes fear among his children represents a "rebellion" against the "staid" moral premises of those innocent people. This creates a conflict between them which leaves them helpless to his anger and arguments.

There is nothing they can do. He makes sure of it. The result is a total disregard for the anxiety and fear of innocent children.

This is what I call the "I need to be free" lie for drinking. The truth of all this is that most drinkers want to ameliorate their pain and moral doubt through a failure that causes each of them to doubt their moral worth. Alcohol drowns all of those doubts so he can "act" and "think" – but they cannot do anything about his drinking. Alcohol helps his mind blank out the pain he is feeling. It cannot help them deal with their pain. The arguments about his need for freedom were bluster and pretense that create conflict and even more self-doubt in everyone within this dysfunctional family.

Likewise, an obese person has similar fears and thinks that gorging on huge meals and snacks is a way to block them. He feels good when he eats because the feeling of having a full stomach is a symbol of the idea that he will never be deprived of the comfort of food. Again, it is the pain that is being blocked by the idea that eating a lot means everything is ok.

Drug users and sex addicts do the same thing. The drug is a very efficient way to feel that life is ok. Even excessive sex makes the person feel that he is loved and not deficient.

These addicts have conditioned their minds to lie to them and the only time they realize they have been lying to themselves is when they are hung over, looking in the mirror, in withdrawal or physically spent. At that point, the lie is obvious and so the solution to the "hangover" is to build up enough strength to start the lying again; and since now they have to deal with the moral and personal aftermath of what they have done to their life, they have to come up with new rationalizations that what they did was not their fault. "I was just drinking. I don't know how it got out of hand."

The network of lies that the addict builds up over his lifetime is still not enough to help him ameliorate his pain (including the new pain he has felt as a result of his "freedom"); so in order to avoid going into the rabbit hole of depression, he supports his lies by choosing people around him who will tell themselves the same lies, which gives him the strength, through their approval, to continue his rationalizations.

This means that he requires fools among those who love him. He requires that they accept his lies and believe them to be true. Eventually, those around him will learn that there is no "getting" to this individual and "there is nothing I can do" to help him. This moves many people to avoid him, steer clear of him and just let him self-destruct. There truly is nothing they can do for him until he realizes that he has been lying to himself.

What causes psychological pain? What gives some people so much discomfort that they are compelled to drown those pains in man-made substances? Now this is the hard part; what they fear most is the opinions of other people – the very opinions they claim not to care about. They fear the idea that someone may disapprove of them and this causes them to do things that make people disapprove of them.

The base problem for many people is that they derive their sense of self-worth, not from themselves but from what other people say and think. The fear of this is so strong that they can't escape it – this is what causes substance abuse – this fear of others is a major source of the pain that the addict must drown out.

In my philosophy[1], this is called being a second-hander. A second-hander is a person who gets his philosophy of life from other people rather than from his own thinking. For a second-hander, the idea of being free to indulge in his addiction is nothing more than a pretense at independence – a fake

---

[1] Objectivism

independence. What is really going on inside of him is anxiety over what he is sure is a negative opinion of him by other people. In response, he pretends it isn't real and that he is normal. He is, in effect, reversing cause and effect. He is trying to "get" a moral label without actually being moral. He is trying to create a front, a façade in front of the world. Worse than this, a second-hander has programmed his mind to constantly lie to him about his own value under the premise that if people believe the façade, then he is a real person. This programming is essentially a shell game, a deception. The only way to escape this predicament is for the individual to de-program himself and begin to build his self on a more solid foundation. He must prevent his mind from lying to him and learn how to start truthing.

Common Lies You Tell your Mind to Tell You

Let's cover some of the more common lies that people often direct their minds to tell them. Remember, these are not truths; they are rationalizations.

You deserve the pleasure activity

When you tell your mind to argue that you deserve the relaxation that comes with your particular addiction, you are telling it to argue that you should take your substance of choice as often as you like. The substance is not about relaxation but about the amelioration of anxiety and the use of pleasure to avoid psychological or physical pain. What you seek is a blank slate to do whatever you want even if it hurts you. You have told your mind to make arguments for the idea that the pleasure choice does not hurt you at all, that you can control it and that you are still in charge of your life, all of which are lies.

You need to connect with this discussion that is going on in your subconscious mind. Most often, you don't even know that this discussion is taking place within you. But it is there and you need to uncover it, watch it, and begin to change the conversation. Here's an example:

At the grocery store, you are walking through the aisle. You see some food that is unhealthful but very delicious. You have gorged on this food in the past and you have told yourself that you should eat less of it. You give yourself the command to tell yourself that you deserve this food and you claim that you have worked hard today and you need something enjoyable. Yet, this food is not for health; it is for pleasure, and more importantly, it adds significantly to your calorie, sugar and cholesterol intake. It is not good for you but you begin to think of the pleasure of eating the food and you are drawn to it as if without choice. You buy the food.

It is here where you need to tell yourself the facts. Too much of this food is not good for you. It can harm you and you have to say "No" to it if you are to regain your health and happiness. Here is where the principle of opposites comes into play. There is a contrast in your mind. Not eating the food is not fun; it doesn't give you pleasure; it is a pleasure-less decision so therefore it must be the wrong decision. When you posit in your mind the decision between eating the food and not eating the food, your mind has all the "reasons" why you should eat the food. Now, you tell yourself why you should not eat the food; such as you will lose weight and begin to feel stronger, have more energy, live longer, not have to work harder to get rid of the weight, etc. The arguments may not win the conversation so you just have to then say "No".

The principle of opposites is a technique for arguing against a bad idea. It is a setting of your mind on the reasons why not doing something is better than doing something you are used to doing by habit. It doesn't matter what you are trying to do that harms you; arguing the opposite can open your mind to new thoughts, new approaches and new outcomes. It is especially helpful in arguing against doing something out of addictive behavior.

You need to memorize this conversation and argue it over and over in your mind until you see the absolute necessity of not eating this food and of buying only the food that you know will help you and especially only in the quantities that your body needs, no more and no less. It is here where constant repetition of his conversation, constantly looking for better and better arguments, and the eventual changing of that conversation to a logical progression of correct thought, helps you to eventually start making the right choices. That is where you can change your behavior – at the point of decisions. Here and only here.

The principle of opposites here seeks to reverse the thinking that rationalizes destructive behavior as moral action (by means of the lies that one deserves the addictive pleasure and that it is natural). When one invokes the opposite idea one begins to justify correct behavior through reason and this can help break the hold that your rationalizations are reasonable. By arguing the opposite, you are arguing that moral actions should be taken when reason supports them according to life as the standard.

Certainly, a deserving person should stand up for the right to have pleasure. But rationalizing the pursuit of pleasure (unrelated to whether the individual has a right to it) is unreasonable. It is a declaration that one deserves pleasure because one is human and therefore anything goes. That is not a prescription for happiness but for disappointment and suffering.

The essence of this approach to change is that one has to replace irrational living and decision-making with rational living and decision-making. But the key is in learning not only what is rational but also what is irrational, being able to identify the key issues. This is why I mentioned here the principle of opposites. This principle can help you argue against doing things that you know to be wrong for you; and it is as easy as taking a contrary view.

So what we are talking about here is making rational thinking and rational decision-making into an active process, one that you practice consistently and with such accuracy that you are able to decide right from wrong for yourself – rather than suffer through irrational thought.

Certainty and morality can only be accomplished by rational thinking and those should be the goals of a person seeking relief from addiction. The opposite of addiction is rational thinking.

If you are able to derive pleasure from rational thought and rational living (and that requires the recognition of the value of rationality and correct action), you can stop living according to your addictions. Once that pleasure takes hold, once it becomes habit (knowledge), you can be guided, almost as by instinct, toward life-serving goals and never fall back on anything so evil, so painful, so harmful as addictive irrational behavior. At that point, you learn that you deserve pleasure – but it is the pleasure of rational living, peace of mind and self-confidence, not the old "pleasure" that derived from a fear of the opinions of others.

The outgrowth of practicing rational thinking and letting it guide you toward rational living is that you are no longer beset by doubt, you earn a sense of living (or a sense of life) that is truly benevolent, happy, proud and self-sufficient. This sense of the good is an accomplishment that can only be achieved by being dedicated to clear thinking, logic and seeing the connection between what is real and what you know.

It harms no one

The justification for "it's not going to hurt me" is not "it's going to help me." The statement that "it's not going to hurt me" is a lie. If it involves your body in any way, in the long-run, it *is* going to hurt you one way or another, either in damage to your relationships or your health (or both).

Some people think their addictive behavior harms no one and they look around for proof of that contention. They see their worried and unhappy children and think they will get over it in a few minutes returning their normal happy selves. If not, they'll take them to the park so they can play. They may think their spouse will always love and support them while constantly searching his or her face to see if the love is still being reflected back. They deny that they have encouraged the spouse to also deny the problems along with them – knowing, deep down, that the expression on their loved one's face is pretended love and fake normalcy.

The denier may look in the mirror at the lines growing on his or her face and think they are just tired or that the process of aging is normal. They may see the extra weight they carry and think it is just a few pounds and they are just pleasantly plump. Or they may not see the extra pounds at all and imagine a svelte frame where there is a huge blob.

If they wind up in jail or prison for committing a drug or other crime, they may blame society for its prudishness and think there is nothing wrong with their integrity. They may develop a disdain for people who would tell other people how to live.

These people live under the delusion that there is no harm in doing harmful behavior. They are constantly in denial about the consequences of their actions. Their drive toward pleasure is so powerful and they are so afraid of the damage they are doing to their minds, bodies and families, that they have to pretend their entire lives. They even pretend that they are special in some way and it is possible to get away with their rationalizations. Yet, the truth is that their addictions have made them un-special, in a sense, and they fear knowing it.

These people have a standing order in their lives. Regardless of what they feel, see or think about the damage they are doing, they deny the truth and pretend that they are exempt from reality. They operate under the principle that if they can think something good about themselves, or if they can make others somehow pretend that there is something special about them, then it must be true. Beautiful conversation over lunch but hardly believable.

The best possible life is to be high (or enjoy your pleasure of choice) all the time

Here, the fallacy is that you can never have too much of a good thing. What the addict has done here is elevated his particular pleasure choice to the position of highest value and this is because he has told his mind to tell them that his life is enriched by feeling this pleasure as much as possible. However, there are some side effects to this reversal of value. It switches cause and effect because pleasure, properly, is the reward for living a good life, not the ultimate value. This:

- Affects your value structure – distorts it because one is always pursuing pleasure rather than a good life
- Can affect your health – loss of sleep, constant excitation, physically overdoing it, etc.
- Causes neglect of other important values and distorts the meaning of happiness

If it feels good its ok

This argument is the hedonist version of morality that declares pleasure to be the motivating factor in human life, either openly or implicitly. It is essentially a rationalization that also ignores the fact that hedonism as morality focuses only on brute physical feeling devoid of intellectual regard. One could say it is the refusal of morality since it declares that brute physical pleasure, as a value, is more important than abstract thought and the ability to survive.

This view ignores the fact that physical pleasure as such is promiscuous and meaningless if it is divorced from a primary value structure. The wind gently blowing the hair on your skin may feel good but without an intellectual argument for its value it is only so much wind blowing by so many hairs. There must be a value for the individual that gives meaning to his life. The mindless pursuit of pleasure without connection to the higher values that proceed from life can never be a higher value.

We all need a little pleasure in life

Certainly, this is true but is that fact a reason to devote your entire life to the pursuit of pleasure? The conclusion people are supposed to draw from it is that it is perfectly normal to spend all your time pursuing pleasure while ignoring important pursuits such as making a living or caring for your family. It is a lie when you tell yourself to ignore your responsibility to yourself as a valuing human being.

The key issue here is knowing the difference between a fundamental value such as life and a derivative value that is less important or disconnected from the fundamental. Pleasure is a derivative value and not a fundamental one. Those who claim that we all need pleasure are doing a disservice to their code of values.

Normal people do it

This lie is a pretense to normalcy for a person who is not living a normal life. But the assertion that normal people drink or engage in other addictive activities is a non sequitur. It makes no difference at all that normal people also do it; the addicted individual is not living a normal life.

Who is Responsible for You?

"I am the one ultimately responsible for my life."[2]

Dr. Ben Carson is a brilliant neurosurgeon who has saved many lives with his innovative

---

[2] Dr. Ben Carson with Cecil Murphy, *Gifted Hands, The Ben Carson Story*, quoted by Don Watkins in *RooseveltCare*

and ground breaking operations. He is a legendary personality who has gained much respect in our society. Yet, his childhood was riddled with trouble, doubt and struggle. What distinguishes him is that he made several key decisions in his life that made a difference for him and the world.

At certain points in his life, when he could have taken that leap into irresponsibility, he made a choice to do something that would have clear benefits and send his life onto a different course. Those choices were not the most immediately pleasurable choices or what seemed right from his gut feeling. Instead, they were long-range choices that had great impact on his future. He refused to take the road of pursuing negative values and chose positive, fundamental values – and that made a difference for him.

The key point for him was not the specific decisions he made, which were good, but the fact that by making choices for himself, he was able to control his life long-range when those choices could pay off.

Although it would be great for an intellectually and morally lazy person if he could have a better life by submitting his decisions into the hands of others, no other person should be given that responsibility. Even if they wanted it, you'd be subject to the decisions of a person who only has responsibility for himself, not for you.

It is best to take ownership of the bad decisions you have made in the past and begin making new decisions upon a different standard. I'd suggest reason and life as the standards. I'm not talking about the lives of others but your life and I'm not talking about the ideas of others but your ideas; thought by you as an outgrowth of looking at reality. You are ultimately responsible for your life.

A standard is something you measure against to determine if a particular action will accomplish what you want. An overall standard could be something like "my life" or "my goals", etc. You want to have a standard with every action you are contemplating. The answer about whether an act meets a standard is a "yes" or a "no". Specific standards might be something measurable such as I need to accomplish 100 sales in two weeks. "100 sales" would be your standard. It is not only a goal to shoot for but, after the two weeks in this case, it is what you use to identify how close or how far beyond your standard you were able to go.

When deciding to drink or not (or to eat or not, etc.) what is your standard and do you consistently pursue that standard? You certainly can't accomplish it if you have given your mind a subconscious order to rationalize that decision so you can pursue a contrary standard such as your addition. What this means is that you want to do something in such a way that it is harmful to you.

Which gets us to the principle that if you arrived at a decision irrationally, then it is immoral and without a standard. So what are correct standards for thinking about your decisions. Needless to say, you have to have an overall standard such as life and then a specific standard such as how a specific value will affect your life.

Once your mind starts telling you the truth, you can develop the standards necessary to control your life and do the right things for yourself. When it comes to the ultimate standard, you have two choices: life or death, living well or living poorly. It is your choice.

The next decision reflects your values in the order of their importance. We'll learn how to do this in Step 2. And, as we'll see, the critical point here is to tell yourself the truth about why these values are good for your life. Get that truth impressed into your mind so it moves to the front of your thinking.

In fact, I won't even argue for why I think life is the standard. You will do much better for yourself by looking around at the world and deciding why life should be the standard and why death should not be the standard. I'd suggest that you write your thinking down on paper so you can look at it later to help you think about your standards while you are in the process of taking an action. As you watch people moving about, talking, working, thinking, eating and living, ask yourself what is the implied standard of their actions.

It is About Attitude

What is attitude? How can it influence your life? How do you get an attitude?

Your attitude is based on a general approach to life. Oftentimes attitude is influenced by life experience and can be understood through careful analysis with the help of a professional. Optimally, your attitude should be positive and self-interested. Living a moral life and experiencing the success that comes from moral living will help create a good attitude. Bad attitude comes from thinking and acting irrationally, without thought and without reason. Bad attitude breeds failure.

Why is moral living the key to attitude? Living according to reason, looking at reality and adhering to it will create success. In a sense, what you do to the best of your ability will come back to you in positive results. It is a simple rule: understand the "is", let it help you determine the "ought" and you will experience the euphoria of positive results. This breeds confidence, peace of mind and happiness – a good attitude.

You can control your attitude but that depends on your overall view of life and living. Your attitude can range from "benevolent" all the way to "malevolent" and it reflects your feelings about how the universe (or reality) is either open or closed to your success in life.

If you have an attitude that reality is a sort of "god" who thinks you are evil, you will tend to be distrustful, brooding, unhappy and often in conflict with others. This attitude can be the source of much anxiety and psychological pain which can often be met with a desire for poor pleasure choices that can become habitual.

If you have an attitude that the universe is open to you and that there are no obstacles to accomplishing your happiness. This means you will experience less psychological pain and there are fewer inducements to drowning your feelings with an addictive substance.

Who/WHAT Do You Love?

Values are the key to getting control of your life and there is a simple logic to knowing and developing your values. If they are based

upon life as the standard rather than short-term feelings, they provide a powerful incentive to "doing the right thing".
To understand why this can be helpful, we must define a value and a dis-value.

A value is that which one "acts to gain and/or keep." This definition is provided by Ayn Rand, an Individualist. It gets to the root of the fact that values are a strong inducement for action. You only act to gain something because you see some benefit in gaining it. And this provides a clue to the thinking of the individual who sees harmful acts as in his self-interest. He does not act to gain and or keep but to lose instead – once he realizes this, he can ask himself what does he really value and how can he gain it.

Yet, the critical factor is how to define what one will seek to gain and or keep. In my book, The Age of Selfishness[3], I showed how an individual stranded on a desert island would go about the process of defining his values. This approach can help readers understand

---

[3] http://amzn.to/2aTR24j

how the human mind works when it must fare for itself.

"My story starts with a massive storm in the middle of the vast Pacific Ocean. My ship has been broken into pieces and gone down. After a few hours of clinging to the rope of a capsized life boat, I find myself on the beach of a small island. The storm is over and I can finally rest. Tired of struggling against the sea, I collapse on the beach before eventually recovering my senses. When I look around, I notice the pieces of my broken ship that have washed up with me. I survey my situation and wonder if I will ever return home. After a few minutes, I realize that I must learn how to survive in my new circumstances.

"Before I can begin working on my survival, I must hold some fundamental ideas that are related to every thought and decision I make. First, I must hold that absolutes exist, that reality is predictable; secondly, I must hold that my mind is capable of identifying reality; and thirdly, I must hold that only I can choose the values that will preserve my life. I am, after all, alone in the world. Only I live in this body and only I think with this mind. No one can do this for me, especially on this lonely island.

"These fundamental ideas are of major importance for me. If I hold that reality is not bound by absolute laws, I cannot count on a predictable environment. If I think my mind is inefficacious, I will have no confidence in my conclusions. And if I don't use my mind, I will not know what to do. How do I get from the need to survive to a knowledge of how to survive? This is the question at the heart of morality. The answer is that I need to identify the values I will pursue while on the island. And these values must secure my survival in an absolute sense; they must actually achieve my survival.

"Ayn Rand identifies values as the foundation of the moral life:

""Value is that which one acts to gain and/ or keep — virtue is the act by which one gains and/ or keeps it. The three cardinal values of the Objectivist ethics — the three values which, together, are the means to and the realization of one's ultimate value, one's own life — are: Reason, Purpose, Self-Esteem, with their three corresponding virtues: Rationality, Productiveness, Pride"[4]

Reason	Purpose	Self-Esteem
Rationality	Productiveness	Pride

"Reason is a wide abstraction that includes all the principles necessary for correct thinking. The process of reasoning is a formal process that makes up what is called rational thinking. The virtue that helps me achieve my purpose is called productiveness which is the practice of "making" or creating the things needed for survival. Self-esteem is both the cause of and the consequence of successful thinking while pride is the result of achieving my purpose through production.

""A process of reason is a process of constant choice in answer to the question: True or False? — Right or Wrong?"[5]

---

[4] The Virtue of Selfishness by Ayn Rand, The Objectivist Ethics

[5] Atlas Shrugged by Ayn Rand

""Productive work is the central purpose of a rational man's life, the central value that integrates and determines the hierarchy of all his other values. Reason is the source, the precondition of his productive work — pride is the result."[6]

"Of prime importance for me on the island is my development and use of concepts. "A 'concept' is a mental integration of two or more perceptual concretes, which are isolated by a process of abstraction and united by means of a specific definition. Every word in man's language, with the exception of proper names, denotes a concept, an abstraction that stands for an unlimited number of concretes of a specific kind. It is by organizing his perceptual material into concepts, and his concepts into wider and still wider concepts that man is able to grasp and retain, to identify and integrate an unlimited amount of knowledge, a knowledge extending beyond the immediate perceptions of any given, immediate moment."[7]

---

[6] The Virtue of Selfishness by Ayn Rand, The Objectivist Ethics

[7] Ibid

"Rand elaborates on an important type of concept which she identifies as value:

""Is the concept of value, of "good or evil" an arbitrary human invention, unrelated to, underived from and unsupported by any facts of reality – or is it based on a metaphysical fact, on an unalterable condition of man's existence? (I use the word "metaphysical" to mean: that which pertains to reality, to the nature of things, to existence.) Does an arbitrary human convention, a mere custom, decree that man must guide his actions by a set of principles – or is there a fact of reality that demands it? Is ethics the province of whims; of personal emotions, social edicts and mystic revelations – or is it the province of reason? Is ethics a subjective luxury – or an objective necessity?"[8]

"My values are derived from and supported by the facts on the island. I experience this need for values most urgently in my hunger pangs and in the discomfort I feel in the heat

---

[8] Ibid

(weather) on the island. I realize that I must act now before these discomforts become insurmountable.

"My discovery of this need to act is a rational judgment. I conclude that "I must act in order to survive" and "I need values in order to act" and "I must create my values as soon as possible." I ask, "What are those values?" This leads to my discovery that I must satisfy my body's basic needs first. I consider this and determine that my immediate values are food, clothing and shelter.

"My next step is to identify as many facts as possible on the island. A fact is an aspect of reality expressed by a statement or proposition. "This is the sand" and "This is a coconut" are examples of some of the facts I discover. I look around the island and identify every fact on the island; the trees, jungle, land, shore, water, food sources, climate and shelter possibilities. I consider the nature of each item and identify which ones will most directly influence my survival. I accomplish this by isolating each item mentally and breaking it down into specific characteristics. Those items with similar characteristics, I give a specific name which helps me hold them in memory as a single mental "unit". Then I relate those named concepts' characteristics to their usefulness as food, clothing and/ or shelter.

"How do I accomplish this? How do I determine whether a particular item is useful? How will I connect fact and value? How will I grasp, retain, identify and integrate each item into my purpose? For this I define principles about how each item can be used and compare it to the standard of "what will help me survive?" For instance, "a coconut contains liquid that can quench my thirst" or "fish in the ocean are edible" are examples of some principles I identify.

"Notice that these principles are cognitive in nature. A principle helps me "see" facts of reality mentally. It helps me identify the characteristics of different entities and relate those characteristics to the accomplishment of a goal or value. It is a fact that I can eat fish and nourish my body. It is a fact that there is food in this environment. It is a fact that I can use a rock to kill a bird or other animal. These facts can only be "seen" conceptually but they are critical to the process of understanding reality; they exist and they help me "see" the way to success in life. The only thing left is to act in a fashion that will secure those entities for me.

"Some principles can be framed as "if/ then" propositions. "If I catch fish, then I can eat" and "If I build a house, then I can protect myself" are examples of some "if/ then" principles that I identify.

"Additionally, the "code of values" I have defined (food, clothing, shelter) is based upon real facts in reality that directly relate to my real needs. The materials for accomplishing these values exist on the island but only I must convert them into values. There is nothing arbitrary or subjective about it. I know that I want to live; I know that I value my life and I know that in order to live I must pursue values. Food, shelter and clothing are those values. These are all truthful statements. It is true that "'Value' is that which one acts to gain and/or keep."[9]

"And: "There is only one fundamental alternative in the universe: existence or nonexistence — and it pertains to a single class of entities; to living organisms."[10]

"As I look around, I discover that some canned goods from the ship have landed on the beach. These will tide me over until I am able to process my own food supplies from the island. I need to think about what I will do once those supplies run out; but in the meantime, these items provide me with the luxury of not having to worry about food for a few days.

"With my food needs temporarily met, I decide to address the values of shelter and clothing. I notice that some luggage items from the ship have reached the shore. I also find my own luggage that contained clothes and toiletries I can use. Among the other pieces of luggage, I find boots, heavy coats and other

---

[9] Ibid

[10] Ibid

items. By evaluating these items against the standard of what it takes for protection from the elements, I narrow them down to those most effective against current weather conditions. Clothing items that don't fit my body are set aside for possible other uses later.

"For shelter, I could select a large tree to sleep under but I see that a tree won't repel high winds, rain or hail. In fact, my clothes are insufficient against harsher weather so I need to think long-range about how to get more protection from the elements.

"Again, I need to use my mind. I notice that the process of thinking, learning, inventing and planning for my own survival is highly pleasurable and I'm beginning to feel the pride that comes from production. In fact, the pleasure I find is so enjoyable that I want to engage in reasoning as much as possible. I realize that my learning has made it possible for me to successfully survive; I am experiencing the tangible success that reason makes possible and it is exhilarating.

"The same types of observations I made

during my fact-finding mission will help me gain additional important knowledge. But now, I must go beyond perception and sensation to create a new concept that I must make with my own hands. This means I must find materials that are useful in the creation of a home. Using a process of induction or trial and error, I can gain knowledge about other items on the island. I examine the more solid, more durable materials and evaluate their specific qualities. This requires observation, testing and planning.

"During my analysis, I notice that the trees have large flat leaves. By dipping them into the ocean, I learn they can repel water and they might be useful on the roof of my soon to be home. I look at the sand on the beach and decide it is not suitable for anything because it is made up of tiny particles that do not adhere to each other. I may decide later, by combining sand with other substances such as water and mud, that I can work the sand into a more durable composition, but this will take time and research that I decide to reserve for later.

"I look at the trees and test one with my

hands. I pound on it with my fist, then with a rock, I strike it to see if it breaks. I try to estimate its weight. I learn that it has some of the qualities I seek but I will have to find a way to transform it for my own use. I need something that will help me cut the tree and mold it into a frame. I look around for a tool that would do the job. I settle on a flat sharp rock. In handling the tree, I discover I can use branches of larger circumference to support my structure and smaller branches to make the walls. I realize I will need fewer stronger branches for the structural points and more of the smaller branches for the walls. I get to work making my vision into a reality.

"Throughout this process, I have invented several new concepts that I had merely taken for granted back in England; a self-made home, a wooden structure, tree branch walls and a rock-tool. Each of these concepts is identified according to its "defining" characteristics and found suitable for a specific purpose. Other concepts I discovered were judged to be useless for my purposes while others had promise for other purposes. I hold each of these concepts in memory by means of a specific name that I apply to each of them.

"I have discovered the importance of defining my concepts accurately. In philosophy, this is called the correspondence theory of truth. I know that my concepts must correspond to their actual natures in reality. Additionally, I not only discover them, but in the case of new concepts, I invent them –all by means of a thought process that connects my values to their actual accomplishment. The correspondence theory is reason's way of making sure I understand reality and that my concepts function as effective cognitive tools. Only by ensuring that my concepts are "realistic" am I able to achieve my purpose.

"Using this thought process, I can project how my home will look, how strong it will be and how well it will stand up to the elements. Since I have no paper or writing implements, I use a thin stick (another tool) to draw an image of my home in the sand. This is my architectural drawing and building plan. I incorporate into this drawing all the principles that will help me build the home, all the "if/ thens". It is a matter of "seeing" with my mind's eye.

"Since I had no experience in house-building back in the world, I am inventing a new field for myself (home building). And my invention of this new concept is totally liberating for me. It will make so much possible for me and even give me rest and peace of mind once it is built. I stop when I realize that I am being totally selfish about my needs and survival. My actions are, indeed, all about me and I realize there is nothing wrong about this; it is good that I survive. Indeed, my self-sufficiency, my resilience and ability to think are necessary. I understand now that there is no other moral standard to apply except my selfish need for survival. My selfishness is based upon my rational choices and only my rational choices. It is true that knowledge, principles and facts are necessary for me to live and enjoy my life. I smile when I realize this important principle. If I love my life, I must build this structure and only rational thinking will make it possible. Rational selfishness is good and the more of it I have, the better. I am energized by this and hurry to improve my circumstances.

"The principle of selfishness (holding my own rational values as top priority) is an important one for me. Alone on this island, there is no question that I am living morally and that only I am the beneficiary of my actions. Properly, morality can only focus on what I, the individual, must think and do "for myself". This will be an important discussion when it comes to identifying the principles of a proper society and it will help me answer the question of what is moral for me to do in society.

"As Ayn Rand writes: "Consciousness — for those living organisms which possess it — is the basic means of survival."[11] For me, the decision to think, the decision to use my conscious mind, is the key to my survival.

"As I am deep into the process of building my new home, I stop and ask myself what would have happened if I had decided not to use my mind once I woke up on the island? This question gets to the core of the connection between facts and values and between reality

---

[11] Ibid

and morality. What would that choice not to think have meant for my self-esteem and especially for my values? What would it have meant for my ability to produce the values necessary for my survival? Who would have provided those values for me without my singular participation? Certainly, a choice not to think would have meant that I had no desire to live or to return home. It truly is an either/ or proposition; either I use my mind or I die.

"The lessons in the above example point out some important facts. In order to live, it is a fact that I must use my mind. It is a fact that I must observe reality. It is a fact, that I must use concepts. I (and you) cannot survive without first thinking, working, doing, inventing and improving. The better use you make of your mind; the better survivor you will be."[12]

So, we must start with the truth that it takes a distorted sense of value in order to have an

---

[12] The Age of Selfishness by Robert Villegas, Being Rationally Selfish – What does it mean?, Softcover, Self-Published Amazon.com

addiction problem. If, on the island, I had thought that my first value was not food, clothing and shelter but instead an available supply of alcohol, something would have been wrong with my system of values and my prospects for survival.

What would I have accomplished on the island by ensuring a supply of alcohol before I considered my needs for food, clothing and shelter? I would certainly have delayed or not even accomplished those critical values upon which my survival depended – especially at a time when they were needed most. Here, in modern society, we can take them for granted because we can pay someone to provide them but still we cannot easily ignore those needs (as many homeless alcoholics have learned). You need to think and you need to work (just like I did on the island) before you can accomplish the values necessary for life – if life is your standard. To pursue a mere pleasure first (like many alcoholics do) is a recipe for a short and unpleasant life.

My ten-step program represents steps you can take to change your mind and give yourself choices about the things you do. You should always be thinking if you intend to control your actions and your life. It is not easy but it is worth it. Eventually, as your thinking progresses, your better thoughts will become subconscious and give you an even stronger power to control your life for the better. I've developed these ten steps over the years as points for myself and they have been very helpful in keeping me from engaging in what I call irrational pleasure choices.

A good place to start is to evaluate your most basic values and then ask yourself which of these values are contradictory to other values. Especially ask which values threaten your life and the accomplishment of your other values. That is where we need to start with the Secular Ten-Step Program.

Part 2. The Ten-step program

Before we get started, there is one caveat. The attraction of some addictions, especially hard drugs, are very powerful and the physical changes they create in your body make them nearly impossible to break. At least, that is the state of our knowledge today. Although I was able to break the hold of alcoholism on my body by concentrating on my mind, the possibility is that with some addictions, the attraction cannot be reversed easily without some professional assistance. I don't recommend that you attempt to deal with hard drug addiction on your own. The twelve-step program may not work when it comes to substances that alter your body chemistry to the degree that hard drugs can alter it.

Additionally, I am not a psychiatrist or counselor by any means. This secular approach is intended to offer you an understanding of how I dealt with my addictions and the kinds of thoughts I had to understand. I heartily suggest that you not follow these steps on your own. You should have help, friends, a good counselor and other professional people who can help you work through the steps. I offer no guarantees nor do I claim to have all the answers.

Until more research is available, I am not making any claims for this twelve-step program. I only offer it as an aid in helping you "change your mind" and not as a panacea or prescription for dealing with any form of addiction. I make no claims for the effectiveness of this program. I only know that it helped me "change my mind". I have not consumed alcohol now for eighteen years and have never had the urge to try it since starting this program. Perhaps it can help you.

Step 1. Liberate yourself

In order to properly direct your life, you must become an independent thinker. I'm not talking about reading every major philosopher, two newspapers a day and five books a week. I'm merely talking about doing the best you can to think with your own mind rather than follow what you are told by so-called authority figures, peers, parents and other family members. Certainly, we love them but you have a responsibility to yourself to get your life right and you have to start with what happens inside your own head.

The key to starting this liberation is to do an assessment of how independent you are regarding decisions you make for your life. Here are a few questions to ask:

1. Do you often change your mind or feel uncomfortable when someone disagrees with you or criticizes something you do?
2. Is your first thought about any issue what other people think rather than what you think?
3. Do you prefer to investigate an issue and study it to define what you think or do you just ask others?

Thinking for yourself is not an easy habit to get into. It requires some basic knowledge of how good thinking is done and even a little bit of courage.

I think that thinking for yourself is essential to defeating addiction. And you will find that it is enjoyable and beneficial to learn to be independent. There are plenty of good books that will teach you how to think clearly and I'd suggest that you buy one or two. You will be glad you did.

The best advice I can give you in the short amount of space we have is to develop the habit of looking at reality first when you have a question. Avoid looking for the opinions of others (unless they are experts in their field) and don't hesitate to ask probing questions and develop your own conclusions.

One thing you should do, at this point, is to read the chapter on theory in the Appendix to this book. Try to understand, as best as you can, that addiction is an approach to pain. As an individual, you have encountered physical and psychological pain and you selected a particular out-of-context approach based upon an emphasis on pleasure in order to deal with the pain.

I would suggest that you use a journal to help you answer these questions:

- How have I habitually used pleasure to deal with my pain?
- What has given me pain?
- What is my physical pain?

- What is my mental pain?
- What caused these?
- How can I change the thinking that requires that I try to escape my pain?
- What can I do to confront my pain and relieve it without addiction?
- What must I change in my own mind in order to understand this process of dealing with pain through acceptance of my addiction?

Keep this journal with you at all times and while you are sitting alone, waiting at the car dealership, sitting in your car on a bench in the park. Spend lots of time on these questions and see where the they lead you? Try to convert your discoveries into actions? As you go through these steps, the answers to your questions will help you have a broader perspective on your problems and help you with the other parts of the ten-step program.

Step 2. Make a list of your values.

I am not going to tell you how to live your life. I will only say this: you have a problem and that problem is derived from how you think.

There are good influences in society and there are bad but the responsibility to "get it right" is yours and yours alone. You have to straighten out the mess. In this book, I have tried to give you some guidelines and ideas on the way forward. I hope you find them helpful.

The most important thing you can do is regain your control of your life and this requires accepting your personal responsibility for doing that. You need to know how to think about you and what you need to do to correct your past mistakes.

You are responsible for yourself. If you make a mistake in thinking, you will also make a mistake in acting. You need to understand how you make your mistakes and, more importantly, you need to understand how to avoid making those mistakes in the future.

How can you do this? It is all about values; the right values; values that clearly benefit your life.

You will find this an interesting exercise that

will give you new insights into your life.

Remember the definition of values as having the standard of life. Now we will engage in a process that helps you define your values, organize them and appreciate their importance for you.

For this step, get out a piece of paper and write down the things you value most in whatever order they come to you. Don't forget values such as your children, loved ones, and your goals such as a college degree or getting a raise, anything that you pursue in order to advance your life, knowledge, happiness, condition of living, etc.

Let's say that after about half an hour, you have come up with the following values:

- My children
- My wife
- A good home
- A promotion at work
- Playing tennis
- Keeping myself fit
- A nice pair of shoes
- A new suit

- New tires for my car
- Helping my mother

Now, before we work on these values, I'd like to suggest that you put at the top a special category of values called "Cardinal Values". I would recommend "reason, purpose and self-esteem[13] as three Cardinal Values that will help you make all the others possible.

Needless to say, you need to give some thought to why you should do this and here's my argument:

If you are going to understand why you want to engage in harmful activities, you need to use your best thinking. In some cases, you are going to have to make an effort to learn how to think so you are no longer lying to yourself. You'll even need to use your mind to understand how to accomplish your values and how to keep from self-destructive behavior. This is reason.

Additionally, you need a clearly defined

---

[13] These are the three cardinal values that Ayn Rand included in her discussion of the topic of values in her book The Virtue of Selfishness. http://amzn.to/2aOPB3q

purpose in life if you are going to put yourself on a path toward success. It may take some effort to define your purpose but you'll find that the effort is well worth it because your purpose can be a beacon that will help you know when you are straying from your overall goal of achieving your ultimate values. Ask yourself what is the over-arching thing that you would like to dedicate your life to accomplishing. What defines you and your life in terms of your ultimate goals? Then distill the answers to a singular purpose (you can also have sub-purposes as well but it is important to limit your main purpose to one fundamental accomplishment).

Finally, you need a sense of self. You have to want to respect and appreciate yourself more than you do at the present time. The likelihood is that your self-esteem is often taking some hits as you continue to engage in your harmful behavior so you need to start building yourself up to help give you a reason to do the right thing for yourself.

With that said, the first thing you should do is to stop thinking in terms of failure or success.

Going off the wagon, so to speak, at least when you are getting started on your quest to regain your life, is not the end of the world. You should learn to treat any "failure" you experience as a chance to learn what is going on in your mind.

When you do go off the wagon, don't excoriate yourself and insult yourself. Examine what was going on in your mind at the time and write it down. Then use it as a reference point the next time you are tempted. Learn to use these "failures" as opportunities to learn about your inner mind so you can understand yourself better. Stop beating yourself up. This is a process not a commandment.

The Cardinal values I suggested above will provide a structure to your value system so you need to think through why you need them and how they will work together to help you plan and organize your life around positive living. Please take whatever time you need to convince yourself. If you have any questions, please check with your counselor.

Hopefully, I've convinced you that these cardinal values should go at the top of your list. To help make them concrete in your mind, you should also add these values: rationality, productiveness, pride like this:

Reason	Purpose	Self-esteem
Rationality	Productiveness	Pride

These additional three values are directly related to the Cardinal values. Rationality is your commitment to think rationally and act rationally. Productiveness is how you will achieve your purpose. You will work, create values to trade with others, develop your work skills, etc. and Pride is the expression of your respect for yourself and how you will conduct yourself in all phases of your life. Now we can turn to your list.

The first thing you want to do with your list is arrange it in the order of importance. Put the most important values at the top of the list and arrange them toward the bottom with the least important value last. Throughout this process, you'll want to add or remove values as you see fit. Again, this is not a legal document so just put things down as you think about them. Later, as you see a need, you can adjust these values or even add additional values.

Here's the list I came up with for you:

Self
- Playing tennis
- Keeping myself fit
- A nice pair of shoes

Family
- My wife
- My children
- New tires for my car
- Helping my mother

Home
- A good home
- A 4K Big Screen TV

Career
- A promotion at work
- A new suit
- A new computer

You'll notice that I've created categories for values that relate to specific contexts. I call these "buckets" but you can call them categories if you'd like. This approach also enables you to concentrate on one category during the context in which you are situated in that context. For instance, you have to work Monday through Friday so you can concentrate on your value hierarchy for "career" during those times. Now that you know which values are most important within that category, you can schedule certain times to focus on creating "to-do lists" that focus on those values. Each sub-value or "step", once it is completed can be scratched off the list so you can move to the next step.

Your "Personal" category may have many more values in it because it represents your own special context for developing yourself, your interests and likes. This is most likely an enjoyable part of your value structure but notice that I've put it at the top and hold it to be the most important category. Of course, this is optional. It really depends on one thing: reality. But, in my view, the reality is that only you can be that important to yourself that you'd want to put yourself first.

That's right, reality. Every one of your values should be tied to reality and related to the standard of what is good for your life. Why is this important? You have to have a clear certainty about your values. You have to know that they are real or can be made real through your productive ability. In fact, a big part of your confusion about your actions and behaviors is related to uncertainty about your values.

If this confuses you, it may be because you have been taught to distrust reality. Yet, Aristotle taught us long ago the essential truth that can help us understand reality. In essence, he said that A is A (the law of identity) and this means that every entity in the world is a distinct entity that can be understood by identifying its characteristics. Add the law of identity to the law of cause and effect and you have the principle that things act according to their distinguishing characteristics in a given context.

Why is this important? What do philosophical issues have to do with your bad habits?

Good questions. The answer is that your

approach to life has a starting point. This means that your understanding of the nature of reality and how to think in the real world are part of your psychological foundation, the two subjects you think about most often without even knowing about it (what is real and how do I know it?). In other words, you are always consumed by two questions in life.

What does this have to do with your bad behavior? What does this have to do with your self-destruction? Everything. Here's why: Before you can decide to pick up that drink, you must have a reason for it. You must know that doing so will accomplish something for you (either good or bad). So you must have an understanding of the nature of reality. It is knowledge of reality that gives you the information that picking up the drink will make you feel better. So the question of what you know and how you know it is critical.

If your core conscious values are positive and defensible; which means you have connected them to reality and they have a clear benefit for you, you can then easily identify those harmful subconscious core values and eliminate them.

So, let's take the next step. Go through your list and find out where your particular addiction is located. Let's make sure it gets on the list because you know, at this point, it is an important value for you and it must be integrated into your core values.

Let's say we come up with this list:

Self
- Playing tennis
- Going to the bar
- Keeping myself fit
- A nice pair of shoes

Family
- My wife
- My children
- A relaxing drink at home
- New tires for my car
- Helping my mother

Home
- A good home
- A 4K Big Screen TV
- A bar

Career
- Enjoying drinks with my fellow workers
- A promotion at work
- A new suit
- A new computer

Regarding your values in the category of "yourself", doesn't "going to the bar" seem out of place? The only way it could not be out of place is if it were not a value. Sitting at a bar for hours and getting drunk takes you away from developing yourself. What is the proper conclusion to draw from this?

How about that relaxing drink at home in your "Family" category? That may not be too bad but it could also be a rationalization that drinking is merely an innocent family activity. Nothing wrong with dad having a drink while the family sits on the couch to watch a movie.

There are several problems with this, not the least of which is what it communicates to your children. This can be especially confusing when they see Dad acting "uncharacteristically" and frequently getting playful, for instance wrestling with the kids and being overly generous when they ask him for a new toy or to go to the local amusement center whereupon Dad may need to drive drunk. Or it could mean your wife getting upset with you because you have blown the family budget in taking the family out.

All of this tells the kids Dad acts differently when he is drinking and sometimes Mom has to carry him to bed because he might fall over. How do all these "benign" family activities disrupt the family and work against your values for your family? Are you going to rationalize them and pretend they don't matter? Perhaps your wife does not rationalize them and thinks less of you as a man.

Now let's look at that bar you'd like to add to your home. Certainly, it implies that you think drinking is something that should be done often in a home. Of course the homes of rich people frequently are populated with classy bars and shiny glasses and a fully stocked cabinet. But do you really wish to spend hours of the day drinking? Do you really plan to have lots of parties with your neighbors and associates?

What about enjoying a drink with your fellow

workers? Of course, you work hard and it is great to wind down the weekend and spend some time relaxing. Yet, have you noticed that some of your fellow workers always say "No" when asked if they'd like to join? Or have you noticed that after one drink other fellow workers go home? And over time, even these fellow workers decide not to participate. Have you noticed that now only a couple of you are left at the bar and that you are both drunk? At some point, your boss notices that you are hungover during the week and he begins to question your production and wonders what is happening with your personal life. Perhaps that harmless drink after work is not so harmless.

After thinking this through, perhaps it is better to remove those "drinking values" from your list and your life. This is not as easy as it seems but you've taken a big step in realizing the truth about drinking and living. You might consider replacing them with some more healthful and positive values.

The process of establishing your values will take time. You should spend lots of time thinking about each of these values, how you will accomplish them, what sub-values they imply and how you will accomplish these as well. This process will help you get your mind straight and help you learn to avoid thinking about non-values and addictions that contradict your values. This means you should be thinking about this list virtually all the time, get it inside of you, and make it your constant thought.

Step 3. Feel your Values

But this is more than just a list. You should learn to experience your values because of their importance in your life. Learn to feel them and how much they mean to you, especially those values that are fundamental to your life, your mind, your needs and especially those people you love. They are not just lines on a piece of paper, they are the reason you live. It can help you tremendously to learn just how deeply you love them and how much they mean to you especially when you compare them to the artificial and poorly chosen disvalues that are harming your life.

See your true values in perspective and put your disvalues in their proper place as unimportant things you really don't value at all.

The critical point for you always comes at the time when your feelings and your reason conflict. Your troublesome emotions are based upon your past faulty thinking; they give you your rationalizations and they drive your body to do what you subconsciously want to do. It feels like your body "needs" the addiction and you have convinced yourself that fighting the "needs" of your body is unhealthful. This is the decision point where you need to confront your bad emotions, question them and defeat them for their irrationality. This will help you create a new decision point that is based upon your self-interest and values.

It is at this point where you need to convince yourself that your emotions are wrong; that they are based upon false premises and at that point of decision, you must say "No" to your desire for the addiction. It is at this point, when you are literally flying blind, driven to the satisfaction of the addiction that you can stop yourself – but you must keep in your mind the fact that now, under the power of the false emotion, you cannot stop yourself. You must engage yourself at every turn when the false emotion is driving you so that the debate within becomes conscious and open; and once you arrive at full consciousness of the irrational decision, you will begin to develop, by means of the principle of opposites, to begin the process of changing your action, basing it on reason, positive, correct facts (knowledge) and this will change your emotion that drives you toward a more positive value and life-serving decision.

The better you get this thought process out into the open, the better for you. The more you engage in the process, the closer you will get to understanding what is going on inside your mind and the better you will be at controlling it and making the right decisions.

Some tips:

1. If you fail, it isn't the end of the world. It merely means that you are programmed too strongly toward your addictive

behavior. You just have to try to do better next time. Mentally record what you thought in that moment of decision and especially make sure your record how strongly your subconscious fought to make you do it. This will serve you well when that moment of decision comes again. You will know what to expect. The more times you make these mental notes, the stronger will be your ability to prepare for what to expect next time so you get everything clear in your mind.

2. You need independence of thought. It is easy to fall back into thinking the way other people think. We've been taught to do that all our lives. But it is critical on this point that you think independently and avoid, as much as possible, following old ways of thinking. It is your life; not the life of other people. It is your mind and you must pave your own path if you are going to understand yourself.

The key point is that moment of decision. It is there where the inner-deception takes place. It is at this moment where you can catch yourself. Ask yourself to be more specific about your reason for choosing the activity. For instance, "Why do you think you need to eat right now?" "Who are you trying to please in consenting to this activity?" Be as precise as you can and try to dig deep into what is going on in your mind. Make it explicit so you can check the facts and argue against it.

Step 4. Stop Lying to Yourself and start Truthing

The basic premise of this step is to realize that, deep down inside, you want your addiction or choice of pleasure. You have given your mind a command to lie to you and you have deliberately agreed to accept that lie by deciding to engage in destructive behavior. This now subconscious desire (emotion) enables actions that are contrary to your chosen values.

As we saw in step two, by defining your values and listing them as we have suggested, you are able to identify contradictions in your values. You also obtain the ability to think about them in explicit terms and this is a big step toward resolving the value contradiction. Now you have to identify the lies that you have told your mind to tell you.

"Once you have validated your moral code, if properly done, you have only the choice to be moral or immoral. If your morality is "for you", your highest amoral maxim is to live life to the fullest. Once you accomplish this, you have no choice but to follow that morality to the extreme. You can't simply say that you'll be moral part of the time or that you'll only be half-moral. You are either moral or you are immoral. And, it is a choice of life or death."[14]

Needless to say, you should look carefully over your value list and try to write down as clearly as possible the contradictions in your values and identify how these contradictions affect your choices. Each contradiction is an indication that your values are at cross-purposes.

Let's examine the contradictions in the list of values we have created. Here's the list again:

---

[14] The Age of Selfishness by Robert Villegas, kindle version, Anti-man

Self

- Playing tennis
- Going to the bar
- Keeping myself fit
- A nice pair of shoes

Family

- My wife
- My children
- A relaxing drink at home
- New tires for my car
- Helping my mother

Home

- A good home
- A 4K Big Screen TV
- A bar

Career

- Enjoying drinks with my fellow workers
- A promotion at work
- A new suit
- A new computer

Doesn't going to the bar conflict with your being fit? Doesn't it make being fit more difficult? You could be playing tennis with that time and you could buy a new pair of shoes with the money that you spent on booze.

But there is always the chance that if you leave the bar drunk and try to drive, you will be arrested by a cop and have to undergo jail, a trial, group therapy, psycho-analysis, possibly even divorce and losing your kids. How could you advance your values for yourself with all of these distractions?

Let's stay on this for a while. I want to go deeper into the arguments (facts) that your mind would seek to find in order to place "going to the bar" into your hierarchy of values. It is with the decision to go to the bar that you are giving your mind the order to find those facts and present them to you as valid reasons why going to the bar is *not* a contradiction of your values.

This is the thought process that you need to isolate and observe so you can get an objective view of what is happening inside your mind. Here is an overview:

1. You found early in life a specific pleasure that helped you evade the requirements of living and/or thinking – it helped you with your fears.

2. You chose this pleasure as a value merely because it made you feel better.
3. You learned that the value was largely considered to be destructive.
4. You told your mind to find "facts" or arguments that enabled you to engage in the pleasurable activity.
5. These arguments became part of your moral code and conflicted with your other positive values.
6. Look at your values and see how some of them contradict each other.
7. Stop telling your mind to lie to you. This is the critical point where you must argue with yourself in order to arrive at a point where the arguments "for" the value are challenged.
8. Argue with yourself every time you find yourself telling your mind to justify these contradictory actions.
9. Develop the habit of truthing and never letting your mind lie to you.
10. As with most things that require skills, repetition of these arguments is critical to your success. Careful note taking of your thoughts can be very helpful.

"Needless to say, there are a great many investigations that an individual will need to make in order to arrive at a point of developing his or her moral code. Metaphysical issues regarding the nature of reality, the ability of man's mind to ascertain reality, the nature of concepts and the reasoning process are issues that each individual should pursue before he can begin to choose the purpose and values he will pursue."[15]

This is why we are here trying to put order to your values. You need your mind to identify your values and how to pursue and acquire them. You need to have a clear picture of what you are working for and why.

So now, let's look at what you left behind in your past. You may not realize this (and this is part of the problem) but there are values which you have probably left off your list.

These are values that you developed very early in life that are now subconscious. These values may contradict your chosen values because they were chosen when you were so young that you don't remember them.

---

[15] The Age of Selfishness by Robert Villegas, kindle version, The Benefits of Being Selfish

Look at what you are doing now to contradict your values list and ask yourself what happened in your past that got you to a point of wanting something that might not have been good for you.

Now that you've gone through a thorough analysis of your values and found the contradictions, you must "automatize" the thought process that will remove the contradictions and create a moral code based in integrity. But this isn't so easy. You still have those earlier arguments that have gone "underground" in your subconscious. Those arguments keep telling you that your contradictions are justified. Look at the list above about how people think about their addictions and how they communicate to their own minds; this is a sort of infinite loop intended to find "facts" and arguments to engage in the harmful pleasures. You need to understand this process thoroughly and use it to monitor your thought process as you seek to change and improve your moral life.

Have this list with you at all times; use a notepad to help you walk through your thought process so you can monitor it at times when you have a moment and would like to keep the process clear in your mind. It will help you gain your moral footing and keep you on track.

You should keep in mind that whenever you do something solely for pleasure, you are more than likely contradicting your other values in some way. For instance, eating for pleasure becomes such a habit that you are constantly eating in violation of your value of being healthy. When you rationalize eating for pleasure because "you deserve it", you are lying to yourself so you can do something that you want to do. That pleasure is more important than your own life and that threatens your life.

This last point is critical because you need to start identifying those things that threaten your life and avoid them like the plague. They must become so odious and distasteful for you that you never want to do them again. Yet, this process only requires that you learn what they are and how harmful they are to your values and life.

A good way of getting the right perspective on your addictive behavior is to realize that you are telling your mind to lie to you about the idea that your addictive behavior is good for you. This is a reversal of correct thinking. If something is, in fact, bad for you, you should not want it. So if you find that you do want it, you must identify the arguments you make that are "working" to keep you doing them and evaluate those arguments for what they are: harmful and even deadly.

Another way of understanding this position (that will help you understand yourself) is to ask yourself a hypothetical question. If your life is going better than you had ever hoped. If everything is happening in your life perfectly and beyond your hopes and dreams and you are incredibly happy with everything and everyone in your life, would you even think about engaging in your addiction of choice? If you knew that your addiction would cause all of your greatest dreams to tumble down like a house of cards, would you even be tempted to engage in it?

The questions can help you clarify just how

dangerous your addiction of choice really is and it should serve as a solid reason why you should stay away from it with certainty and conviction.

You should learn to argue with yourself. For instance, late one night when you decide you want a muffin and a cup of hot cocoa, you should realize that you don't need them and are putting additional calories, sugars, cholesterol and other chemicals into your body and harming your health. By arguing with yourself, you can find reasons why eating now is harming. You may not always win this argument but it is important to keep arguing until you start winning.

As I mentioned before, at this early stage, it is not necessary to prevent yourself from having these urges. They are the result of your body's craving the addiction. The important thing is not to "guilt" yourself. What will eventually stop you is when you have completely "undone" your rationalizations through reason. At that point, the urges will dissipate. It won't be easy but it may not be as hard as you think as long as you keep using your mind.

Step 5. The Principle of Opposites

Another way to deal with these
subconscious arguments about your
pleasure choices is to use the principle of
opposites. Simply put it means taking a
bad thought and thinking in reverse, in
its opposite.

This method can be particularly effective
when you are trying to rationalize
positive arguments for harmful behavior.
It involves:
1. Knowing that your arguments for violating
   your values are wrong.
2. Knowing that they are subconscious and
   difficult to excise.
3. Saying the opposite of the false argument and
   emphasizing it emotionally by thinking of the
   negative nature of the consequences of
   defending the action.
4. Repeating the argument as many times as
   possible.
5. Developing a distaste for the addiction.

Once you have identified a good argument against the addiction (using this method), write down the argument in simple terms in your notebook and refer to it when you are alone or waiting at the dealership for your car to be repaired or standing in line somewhere. The key here is repetition and improvement of the argument.

Let's look at an example:

When my mind lies to me that it is perfectly normal to go to the bar at any time, those arguments can be met by the opposite argument: going to the bar is irrational, it is not normal, it is dangerous if I drink too much and get arrested, my children don't like seeing me come home drunk. These arguments are actually better than lying to yourself. They are the anti-thesis of the lies you tell yourself, and in this case, they are the truth. Write them all down in your diary.

Telling yourself the opposite of your rationalization is one way that you can discover that you are lying to yourself. Get into the habit of doing this and you'll find that, over time, you'll have less incentive to go to the bar and more incentive to do positive things like teach your boys/girls how to play ball and give them the attention they need and deserve.

An equally effective attitude is to draw the worst possible picture you can of the consequences of "going to the bar". See yourself as knockout drunk, teetering while you walk, bumping into a door, having an accident. Exaggeration here is not even a lie – it may, in fact, actually happen (or has already happened). Do you really want to live like this? Keep asking yourself that question.

The principle of opposites can provide a glimpse into just how much your mind is lying to you and just how much you want it to lie to you. It can help you, over time, stop lying to yourself and improve your view of reality. The key is to use it effectively.

One key point, and one which will help you make decisions, is that any thought process that leads to your doing the irrational, is immoral – it is harmful to you. What is the connection between the decision and the action?

Essentially, the irrational is the wrong. It is based upon thoughts and ideas that contradict reality and because so it leads you into actions that are wrong or harmful. The irrational escapes being truthful because it is not arrived at by means of logic, clear definitions or realistic observations.

The irrational is anti-logic and anti-mind. It harms you because you do not see the damage it can do to you. You have either rationalized your conclusions based upon your emotions or you desire to have something that you do not deserve. The irrational always leads to a reversal of cause and effect and this means you are seeking the undeserved. The irrational also violates the code of morality that you establish for yourself by means of your best thought and desire for the good (your good). The irrational can also put others above you and send you on the path of trying to please them rather than follow your own logic. Whenever emotions come before reason, you are following the irrational.

Another aspect of this issue is the decision to take a chance or what is often called "a bold leap". It is certainly true that sometimes taking a chance works but it should not be that difficult to know what is right. This is because deciding what is right involves all your values as an integrated unit. If you find yourself in a position of doubt, ask yourself a basic question: "What do I love?" as it relates to this choice. This can often help set the correct context for a proper decision.

Step 6. Learn to See Reality

The key with this step is to know the difference between true knowledge (realism) and false knowledge (rationalizations). Once you acquire this ability, you can then begin to base your actions on truth rather than falsehood.

I've written elsewhere that reason is "cognitive" in nature. When I say "cognitive", I mean that human thinking has the goal of understanding reality as it is. In other words, when you say "I see a table" you mean that you actually see the object that is defined as a "four-legged object with a flat surface". Apply this principle to your entire range of experience and you can understand that you can see reality as it is. This has important meaning for your quest to understand your addictions.

You might have been taught that the mind is incapable of judging and knowing reality but this view is part of the problem. How can a person "know" that drinking too much is bad; how can he know it with his mind if he has no confidence in his mind's ability to know? The first thing to recognize about commonly accepted pleasure choices is that many influences work against your understanding of how to make your own decisions. Advertising, television and movies provide a number of "arguments" for why it is good to engage in "out-of-context" pleasure pursuits. These arguments provide rationalizations for the pursuit of pleasure by attaching irresponsible behavior to "coolness" and "rebellion" – all of which lead impressionable people astray. It is up to you to straighten out the mess you have accepted into your life. You can only do this by questioning everything you have been taught and getting the issues straight in your mind.

At some point, you'll have to take a stand regarding the issue of what is real and what is not. You must then move from what is real to what is morally proper. The second should be based upon the first. Every is implies an ought. Without the "is", you will never arrive at the ought and you'll be perennially tied to the uncertainty which is the foundation of addiction.

I learned that establishing knowledge today is very difficult because both religion and modern philosophy are bent on ensuring that you are confused about the nature of what is real. Yet, that knowledge is what you need in order to understand the world and how your problems fit in.

So what should you do? Challenge your family, your teachers, your professors and everyone you have known in your life? They all tell you they are certain there is no such thing as certainty. Yet, your mind *is* capable of understanding reality. There are certain truths that hold and it is possible for you to discover those truths. Existence exists and it is the job of your mind to understand it.[16]

If you were to take a walk around your local community and then identify some key things that you see, you could ask yourself such questions as:

- Is it real?
- How do I know it?
- How can I discover it?
- How does it relate to all other real things in my surroundings?
- How does it relate to the actions I need to take to advance my life and happiness?

I did such a walk today and made note of my thoughts.

"Just passed by an area that has a little stream that looks to be man-made. The stream feeds into a small pool in which water overflows into another small pool and then another and another. It is quite lovely and peaceful. I see a picnic table by the lake and am immediately

---

[16] I am not the first person to say this. Ayn Rand developed an entire philosophy of life around these propositions.

drawn to the serenity of the scene. Each pool is circled by light grey stones, all the same color and even the lake is circled by them.

"I look up and see the trail of a jet coming in my direction over 30,000 feet above me. I think of the people in that jet – it too is man-made and enables people to travel long distances in a short time. The men who made the jet had to understand engineering, aerodynamics and a whole host of other fields in order to create the plane. Those people on the plane are sitting comfortably thousands of feet in the air. They are dependent upon the quality of the thinking that made that jet. I'm amazed that a small little dot (me) can think of all this and connect the lake and the plane and all the apartments around me to the principles of existence.

"For instance, the ponds and small lakes exist in reality. They are real, solid, entities. They are not miracles, ghosts, demons or spirits. They operate according to principles that can be defined and counted upon to function according to the principle of cause and effect.

The same is true for each element of the scene, the gray rocks, the land, the water, the lake.

They are all real. Stones will do what stones do, water what water does, picnic tables what picnic tables do, etc.

"Everywhere I look, I see the truth of this. If I learn the correct principles, I can see reality and use it to advance my life in the very same way the builders of the lake and the plane used the correct principles to create their specific "thing". There is no mystery; no intellectual incompetence and no magic involved."

What is the conclusion that I draw from this walk today? My philosophical role model said it best: "Existence exists — and the act of grasping that statement implies two corollary axioms: that something exists which one perceives and that one exists possessing consciousness, consciousness being the faculty of perceiving that which exists."[17]

Rather than wonder who you should please and for whom you should give up your happiness, your goal should be to develop a certainty about the nature of reality and using

---

[17] Ayn Rand, Galt's Speech, Atlas Shrugged

your knowledge to identify your values and how you will accomplish them.

Step 7. Understand how Values can be Distorted

Recall the work we did on your values. Step 7 builds upon this. It revolves around the idea that you are addicted to the excessive, out of context and harmful pursuit of pleasures that violates your values. You must understand how your values are being distorted by arguments that tell you it is "ok" to pursue those excessive pleasures. This is where you take ownership of your values and give yourself the true reasons why you should modulate and control your pleasures.

To get there, you must understand the true role of pleasure in life so you can analyze where you are going wrong.

Pleasure is something you need; pleasure is a value that signifies a moral life, or at the very least, that you are living in a condition in which pleasure is one of the rewards. Pleasure has an antipode which is pain. Both are built into the human body as signals through which the body communicates whether one is living well or not.

As we have pointed out, when we are young we sometimes become attracted to a particular form of pleasure and want to experience it as much as possible. Because of our inexperience, we are often not able to put pleasure in its proper context as a value and instead wrongly decide that the more pleasure (of a certain type) that we experience, the better.

In those early days, the idea that the pleasure is good is seen as a foregone conclusion and you accept it without question as a fact. You are simply too young and inexperienced to know better. Later, when you should know better, you see the signs that the value conflicts with other values and sometimes other people. This is when you give your mind the order to find all the reasons why the pleasure is preferable to living a normal life. When experiencing that pleasure requires that you lie to yourself, your life gets distorted by the experience and the singular pleasure becomes your prime value over other high values. You descend into the depths of "low value" living.

The first thing to realize is that your value structure has been distorted by an over-emphasis on derivative pleasure values. We showed this clearly through the process of developing your values when we inserted certain pleasure choices into the list of values.

Pleasure, as such, is derived from mere sensations without intellectual content. Pleasure does not require values or intellectual content until the individual has developed the ability to conceptualize his values intellectually. The adult individual is then able to engage in reason which helps him establish a foundation of values without the need to pursue pleasure for its own sake. At this point, pleasure becomes integrated into the individual's value structure.

Values are not apples on a tree that can be plucked and enjoyed (I do love apples); they are intellectual products of your mind. Real values, values that are truly beneficial and go beyond immediate gratification. To live a better life, you must advance your thinking toward the intellectual and the real. Values are good for you in reality long-term – but it takes your mind and consistent action to make them real.

The key for you is to identify when you lie to yourself. This could include lying to justify drinking, using drugs, eating too much, watching too much television, having too much sex and any number of activities that result in a distorted value structure.

Next, you should consciously reject your subconscious value structure. If you feel the urge to engage in pleasurable activity, you must debate how excessive pleasure choices sabotage your value structure.

Then, you have to re-affirm the reasons for your value structure and see clearly the damage being done to it by an out of context focus on pleasure. This is a positive process but it takes practice and conviction. It takes the certainty that a good value structure is the best and only way that one can accomplish more certitude and happiness.

Next, you must repeat your argument daily

until you understand that violating your value structure is as dangerous as death, that it is evil and that it could destroy your life.

Convince yourself that going-outside-your-value context is distasteful, low and crass and you're starting to get it. You must consider the violation of your integrity to be a grave assault on your life and your happiness; so grave that to do it would be the epitome of stupidity and evil.

Consider what this means. Smoking is dangerous, it smells bad, yellows your teeth and you could die from it. Your lungs get filled up with smoke and dangerous particles that block your air passages; you are susceptible to more colds and other diseases; you harm not only your lungs but your blood circulation and you could shorten your life. Get the picture?

How about drinking? You could get arrested and go to jail which would embarrass you with your family and friends. You could lose your job. You could kill someone or you might do things so terrible that you would destroy your reputation and your present living standard. Drinking and driving could completely destroy your life; you could die or spend the rest of your life digging out from the mess you have made.

Make these arguments as starkly realistic as possible and see the true evil outcomes that could plague your life forever. You could die a failure while your children hate you for what you have done to them. Your wife will no longer respect you, not want to make love to you, even divorce you and throw you out on the street.

To overcome all the lies that you tell yourself takes discipline and thought. It takes clear thinking and logic in order to see the real benefits of your values and the real dangers of your subconscious adherence to false values. You should "know" your values and clearly see their impact on your life.

The difference between pursuing rational values and acting irrationally is an important distinction to keep in mind. For instance, let's look at sex. Sex is, for most people, something their body tells them feels good. In fact, it feels very good especially if you have sex with someone with whom you share values, experiences and ideas. Sex is fabulous. But finding an optimized sexual experience can be difficult. Sometimes it depends on how comely you are, if you are sexually desirable, sexually competent and, more importantly, if you find a person for whom sex is a reward rather than just a thing you do.

If sex is just a thing you do, rather than a deeply enjoyable value that accompanies other high values, then it tends to be promiscuous, meaningless, cynical and addictive. Thinking that sex for the sake of sex is a good thing is the first lie you tell yourself. The lie of casual sex can be very compelling but it leads to a dead end because it is limited in its meaning and benefits.

I am not a psychologist so I don't know if it is possible, once one has gone through addiction, to ever have a "natural" value structure. The thought process and lies that led to addiction, cannot be easily displaced. This is why I think one has to completely eliminate the pleasure addiction by avoiding the act all together first.

You might call it going cold turkey but certainly there has to be a period during which the individual regains control over his or her actions regarding the addiction.

Step 8. Know what Addiction is

In my view, addiction is not merely physical; rather it is also mental and especially emotional. It has an intellectual component that is more powerful than the mere physical attraction of pleasure. *Addiction is an excuse for telling your mind to tell your body that it needs your pleasure choice and that you have no choice about it.* It is your subconscious mind telling your conscious mind that your chosen pleasure is necessary. At the same time your mind is telling you that you are not addicted and that you have control of your life.

Why do I say it that way? Why do I say you are telling your mind to tell your body that it needs your pleasure of choice? I say it this way because I want to make it clear that you are engaged in a form of "sleight of hand" with your own mind. In a sense, it is a form of dishonesty through disintegration of your mind.

When you want to do something you should not do, you sense that you need a way to justify your choice. You experience the feeling of being wrong so you need to be able to tell yourself *subconsciously* that you should convince yourself that it is not really bad. This subconscious thought process is difficult to detect through introspection.

By connecting your judgment to reality, you provide yourself with a powerful tool to understanding what drives you to your addictions. By observing what you are doing subconsciously, you will be able to gain control over those thought processes and see where you are going wrong. Then, when you next arrive at a decision point, you will be able to understand and control how you are deceiving yourself. With practice, you can gain control of those decision events and begin to make correct decisions based upon your values.

This book also provides you with valuable tips to helping you understand the process you use to justify harming yourself. Understanding how other people have dealt with addiction can help you see the process from the outside so you can compare the experiences of others to your own. Look over the story in this volume, *The World's First Drunk* and try to find a group whose professional leader operates according to similar principles.

Step 9. Stop Bad Relationships

One of the best things you can do for yourself is to get certain people out of your life. These are people who engage in bad behavior with you, people who support your rationalizations and encourage you to engage in your addiction.

Face it, these people are not going to help you improve your life. They are only going to make it harder for you to decide about correct action because they are constantly sharing your addiction with you. Remember, these people are addicted too, and they, like you are often teetering on a precipice easily swayed and often unable to resist the addiction which you have shared with them. You each represent the "tipping point" for each other and it is much better for you and him/her if you do not expose yourselves to that point.

It could be helpful to both of you that you explain to your friend that you have made the decision to avoid him because you want to eliminate, as much as surprised to find out that he is struggling in the same way. So, in some cases, the two of you might be able to agree that seeing each other can be harmful.

On the other hand, there is absolutely no problem with just removing these people from your life, don't call them, don't meet them out, don't even engage in conversation with them. You will be much better off without them.

Step 10. Now Start Again

One thing I discovered after I had stopped drinking was that the process of dealing with my addiction was not over. In fact, I learned that I had more than one addiction and that my eliminating one of them caused my addictive behavior to migrate to another form.

You may find that after you have made

significant progress in your addiction to alcohol, for example, you migrate to eating more food or having more sex or smoking more marijuana.

Addiction can migrate from one substance or activity to another. This is because it is a thought process that affects all of the individual's thinking. It is a premise that influences all premises that involve human action. As such, addition will find a place in any part of a man's value structure in which he engages, in faulty thinking. Remember, the process is subconscious and any anti-value you have accepted will rise to the surface and take over when one anti-value is exposed and eliminated.

But now you have the tools you need to examine and explore this new area and correct your thinking. Again, remember that you have subconsciously chosen this next phase of your addiction. You now have the tools to help you understand what you are doing with your mind and you can defeat this addiction and the next if necessary. Once you have identified the next addiction, you need only start over with Step 1.

These ten steps can provide you with a foundation upon which to base your escape from addiction. It enables you to develop a strong value-base that becomes like a solid rock upon which you can base your life and find happiness. It is not an easy road but thinking and knowing are never easy.

Part 3. The World's First Drunk

This story is a fictional telling of the life of the Stone Age man who invented alcohol. Learn about the effects that alcohol had on this man's thinking processes, his social life, family life and financial life. This part of the book is intended as an object lesson on the harm and dangers of excessive alcohol consumption written by a person who grappled with these issues for years.

"Today was an incredible day! I feel great! Today I discovered something wonderful."

"You seem different. Your eyes seem different. Why are you smiling so strangely?" said Shela, my wife.

"I was out looking for grapes, like you told me. And just like I always do, I eat while I pick. Let me look at myself."

I ran to the water hole by our hut to see my reflection, to see if I looked different. I was smiling such a large smile that my face was contorted and red. But I felt pleasant. I enjoyed it. I continued my story to her.

"So today, I was picking from the vines that grow low to the ground, the nice large grapes. I noticed they were somewhat shriveled. I thought they might not be good for eating, so I tasted a few to see if they were all right. They tasted sweeter than fully ripe grapes, so I kept picking and eating. I have some for you in the basket. Anyway, after a few minutes, I started getting this new feeling. My face lit up, getting warmer and warmer, and I began to feel happy."

Shela went toward the basket to look at the grapes. "They are the same kind of grapes we always eat. Just a little shriveled. Why would they make you feel different?"

"Maybe something happens to them, some sort of magic. I don't know. Try some."

She reached into the basket and began eating. After a few minutes, her face began contortions.

"You're right. I do feel different. Very happy.

This is great!"

For a few minutes, we looked at each other, both happy at what we had discovered, and happy because of how we felt.

"Maybe if I have more," I said, "I will be even happier."

I ate more grapes, and it was true; the more I ate, the happier I got. Soon the basket was empty. I stumbled down to the vines where the grapes grew--to pick more. I went back to the hut with my basket full. But this time, I ate only a few grapes and started getting dizzy. The hut was spinning around me. I fell asleep. The next morning, I felt strange. It was the opposite of the happiness from the day before. I was sick. When I touched my head, it throbbed. I wanted to go back to sleep. I felt pain everywhere. Shela said she felt the same way.

I don't understand how this could have happened.

But a few hours later, I felt fine. I began to

think again about how the grapes had made me feel so good. What kind of magic caused this strange happiness? I went back to the vines to see if I could discover their magic. At first, I picked some grapes that were normal, perfectly ripe. When I ate these, I did not get the feeling. But when I ate the shriveled grapes, after only a few minutes, I began to feel light-headed again.

I went back home to tell Shela about my discovery.

"Well," she said. "I don't want to eat grapes that make me feel sick the next day. We have children to feed. We forgot to feed the children yesterday because we were both so happy from those grapes."

"Well, fine," I said. "Do what you want. But this is a great discovery. I enjoyed being happy last night. It was the greatest feeling I have ever had. I intend to get it as often as I can. I'll probably become famous as the man who discovered shriveled grapes." She looked away, and I could tell she was not happy with my words.

Later that day, I got the idea of picking ripe grapes and putting them in the sun to shrivel. I thought that the magic might work better if I separated them from the vine where they could not grow. It worked. After a few days, I tried the grapes I had laid out, and got a most tremendous feeling. I spent that evening happy.

I noticed Shela looking at me strangely while I lay plastered by the fire. She asked me if I wanted to eat, and I told her I was too happy to eat.

The next day, I woke up with the bad feelings again. I knew they would go away soon, so I slept a little longer. Shela worked around the hut and fed the kids. Everything was fine when I awoke, except that she didn't say a word to me.

A few days later, I told my friend Herb about the shriveled grapes. We ate some and got happy together. He loved them more than I loved them. He staggered over to get our friend Biln who was our jingo partner. After Biln had eaten some grapes, he suggested we eat while we played jingo. We tried it, and laughed so hard we didn't notice who had won the game.

Herb came up with the idea to call our new feeling by a name. He said "happy" was too tame a word. He felt that "drunk" was a better word. We roared with laughter when he said it because the word rolled off his tongue in the silliest way.

"Druunnk," he said. We all said it, and it rolled off our tongues the same way. After our jingo game, we each stumbled home. This was the best jingo game we ever had!

On the way home, I stumbled into a neighbor's hut and knocked down a whole wall. When the neighbor saw it, he was very angry and told me I would have to fix it. He took me to the village elder and asked for a resolution. The village elder told me that I would have to fix the hut at my own expense. Now I have to spend a day not drinking so I can think straight and fix his hut. I'm sure Shela will be angry with me too. The village elder said that I should not drink and walk home at the same time. But it was only an accident and could have happened to anyone. I'll take my chances. It probably won't happen again. Besides, who are they to tell me how to live my life?

When I got home, I noticed that Shela was violently angry. She threw a pan at me after I walked through the door. I asked her what was wrong, and she said she had been working around the hut all day while I was getting happy. I told her that "drunk" was the correct word. Nevertheless, she said, she was doing my work while I was getting "drunk." She was not going to put up with it forever, she warned.

"Do what you want," I replied. "I am having fun. If getting drunk feels good, it is good to get drunk. A person should do what feels good. There is nothing you can do about it." The next day, after I got well, I went to see Herb. He was still in bed. Apparently, he had eaten more grapes than I. His wife, Alla, was very worried. She did not know that eating shriveled grapes had made him sick. So I did not tell her.

I went over to Biln's house to see if he wanted to eat some more grapes. He told me that he could not because he was working on a way to drink the grapes.

"That's a strange idea," I said. "It can't possibly work. Everyone knows you have to eat grapes."

"I am going to take ripe grapes and grind them up so they make a liquid. I'll put the liquid in a drinking vessel and cork it up. Then I'll leave it in the sun. We should be able to drink the grapes and still get drunk."

I thought it was a silly idea.

I staggered home that night and waited for Shela to throw a pan at me. This one caught me on the chin. I reacted with a feverish anger, picked up the pan and struck her on the head. That showed her who was boss. The kids woke up and started crying. Had it not been for their crying, I would have struck her again.

The next morning, she woke me up.

"When do you plan on getting back to normal life?" she asked.

"Why do you ask?" I said, rubbing my chin and my head.

"Well, there's a bump on my head. The children are afraid of you now. There is no meat for eating. The yard is a mess and hasn't been tended for weeks. The hut has a hole in the roof, and someone needs to fix it. Are we going to get back to a normal life?"

"Sure. Fix it yourself," I said. "I'll do what I want. Besides, you threw the pan at me. Tonight is my jingo night. I'll be home when I'm ready." I walked out of the hut.

I have never played jingo with a woman. But Herb brought a woman from the other village named Sonda. He had been telling her about our grapes and she was eager to try them. What a wild night! When we were all drunk, we laughed and told the loudest most raucous jokes. We even found a new way to play jingo. The loser had to remove an item of clothing. Sonda lost. Jingo is now more fun than ever.

Sonda and I got to liking each other. I could tell by the way she was looking at me. She said I was a great man because of my discovery. I don't remember getting home. I don't even know if Shela threw a pan at me. The first thing I remembered was that she and the kids were gone when I awoke. I went over to Herb's hut.

I found him and Sonda together in his bed. His wife was away for the weekend. Sonda thanked me for discovering the grapes. She felt privileged to have met a man who had made such a great discovery. She gave me that look again.

Biln came over with his first container of crushed grapes. We all drank it. Herb and Sonda liked the idea of drinking the grapes. Sonda seemed very impressed with Biln and started giving him the looks she had given me only a few moments before. She called him a great man. I was jealous that he thought of drinking the grapes first. Who does he think he is to improve on my discovery?
"Now we are getting drunk the right way." said Herb with a slurred voice. "We drank and

we are drunk." They laughed loudly.

I remember getting mad at Herb over Sonda. I became irritated when I saw her in his bed that day--but did not say anything until I was drunk. I had never argued with Herb before. I also got angry at Biln because he planned on selling his liquid grapes in the market plaza and Sonda now seemed to like him. He would get rich and I would not.

I guess being drunk makes you do things before you can stop yourself. I hit Herb with a drinking cup and opened his head. Sonda grabbed me fiercely by the hair and threw me out of the hut. I fell hard on my face, causing my nose to bleed. I didn't know she was that strong. Had I not been drunk, she could never have done it. So what, I didn't like her anyway. I'll find new drinking buddies.

The next day Biln took his drinking grapes to the market plaza. He told everyone that the liquid would make them happy. He sold all of it. That night many people came to his hut demanding more. He told them he was already preparing tomorrow's grapes. They threatened to kill him if he could not make more. Nevertheless, he was excited about the idea of selling his liquid grapes.

Shela and the kids left me. They moved back to her father's hut. A few days later, he came to talk to me.

"She says you are worthless. Since you discovered the grapes, you have done nothing but get drunk. You do not attend to her or the children. You shun your responsibilities and you blame her for this situation that is your fault. And worst of all, you beat and bully her. You are a drunk. I'm sorry for her because of what you have put her through. I am sad most for the children. They will have to grow up knowing their father is the world's first drunk. I hope they do not follow in your ways."

"But I am a great man," I said. "I'm the man who discovered shriveled grapes. I have given the world happiness. You do not appreciate my worth."

"You have violated nature's most important law. There is no greatness in that. You must understand that your mind is your most needed faculty. Your grapes destroy the mind. Many people have already discovered that and are wise enough to avoid the grapes. Don't you realize what you have lost?"

"My family?" I asked.

"You have lost that and much more: you have lost your soul. I hope you get it back someday. Until you do, good bye."

He walked out the door. I didn't worry about it. After all, my head was hurting. He had always tried to ruin my marriage. Now he had taken my family from me. It was his plan all along. My drinking had nothing to do with it.

These events happened several years ago. The world has changed greatly since my discovery. Men drink the juice when they eat, and they drink it during festivals. It makes every event merry. I have heard that our King drinks until he falls over dead drunk.

Herb and I never see each other. His wife left him when she found out about his drinking. But he stopped and she returned.

And he stopped seeing Sonda. She will now go with any man who has liquid grapes. But she won't associate with me because I know she's a drunk. I'm not afraid to tell her so. Biln is a rich man. He makes 500 gallons of liquid grapes a day and sells it for a high price. Men pay it. But he does not drink the grapes. Most of the women in our village hate him and spit in his path. He does not care.

There are many others selling the juice that is now called wine. And there are many getting drunk. If others do it, then it can't be bad. Biln tells people he discovered the shriveled grapes while picking fruit one day. Everyone believes him and he is hailed as a great man, the discoverer of shriveled grapes. I am known as the world's first drunk. I hate him. He is rich. I am poor. I know he is plotting against me.

Shela has married another man. He does not drink wine. I hate her for deserting me at the moment of my greatest triumph. I hate her for not eating shriveled grapes with me after that first night. That was her mistake in our marriage. People can be so cruel.

The medicine doctor says I will die soon. He says it is from drinking too much wine. I don't believe him and I refuse to stop drinking. What does a witch doctor know?

Last evening, I got violently sick when, for a laugh, some prankish boys served me water instead of wine. My body could not take the shock. So much for drinking buddies.

Everyone looks at me as if my life is a sad tale. They say it is terrible what too much wine can do to a man. But I say this, and will say it until my dying breath: No one...no one can tell you it is bad to have a good time. When you drink, you are happy and can do whatever you want. When you drink, you are a better person. Why should you stop? What's so bad about that? I don't care what they say. When I die, right thinking people, people like me, will say "Nobody told that man how to live."

As I lie here, I begin to remember what life was like before I made my great discovery. I suddenly remember how much I love Shela and my children. What if I had lived my life another way? I look around the room and wonder why everyone looks at me with remorse. My children are lowering their heads. Where is my lovely Shela? I am trying to speak, but cannot. Why are you putting your hand over my eyes? I want to tell them that my life has been.......

Quiz on The World's First Drunk

The test below can be used as the foundation for group session discussions after the test. See the entire document below. You are free to print and use this document in group sessions as long as all links and copyright information is maintained.

Name _____

Date _____

1. What was this man's unspoken final thought? Can you finish his sentence? What do you think he was about to say? Here are some possibilities. You decide. Circle your answer/s

"I want to tell them that my life has been........"
- a wonderful experience.
- a waste.
- a life of accomplishment.
- lived according to my own principles.
- a rationalization.
- nothing but bad luck.

Your answer: _____

2. "Maybe if I have more, I will be even happier." Early in this person's use of alcohol, he discovered that the more he drank, the more drunk he became. This created a desire on his part to drink as much as possible. What was the result of this thought in his relationship with his wife?

_____

_____

_____

_____

_____

3. The first hangover. When he had his first hangover, his reaction was to notice when the pain ended and then he started thinking about getting drunk again. His wife, on the other hand, discovered the losses from this state and resolved to avoid it. What were those losses?

_____

_____

_____

_____

_____

_____

4. "I intend to get it as often as I can." This is his decision after discovering the alcoholic state. At this point, a factor outside his control takes over his life. What is that factor?

_____

_____

_____

_____

5. "But it was only an accident and could have happened to anyone. I'll take my chances. It probably won't happen again." Taking chances on walking home drunk (or driving home today) is common among people who drink. Why is this a bad idea?

_____

_____

_____

_____

_____

_____

_____

6. The first dysfunctional family. List the things that happened in this story that point to the breakdown of normal family relations.

_____

_____

_____

_____

_____

_____

_____

_____

7. Herb was the World's first drinking buddy. When two people drink large amounts of alcohol together, what can happen to their friendship?

_____

_____

_____

_____

_____

8. Moral choices: "I'll do what I want." This idea puts a person at odds with the responsibilities he/she has chosen and with the people to whom he/she has made commitments. What rationalizations (false justifications) would one have to think in order to allow him/herself to "do what I want?"

_____

_____

_____

_____

_____

_____

_____

_____

9. Doing things before you can stop yourself. Why couldn't this man control himself while he was drinking heavily?

_____

_____

_____

_____

_____

_____

_____

10. "...you blame her for this situation that is your fault." When a person must confront the problems drinking has caused, an easy thing to do is make up a "believable" rationalization. What were some of this man's rationalizations?

_____

_____

_____

_____

_____

_____

_____

11. Nature's most important law. "You must understand that your mind is your most needed faculty." Why is this so? List examples and reasons why this is so.

_____

_____

_____

_____

_____

_____

_____

12. How does excessive alcohol use violate "Nature's most important law?" List examples below.

_____

_____

_____

_____

_____

_____

_____

_____

13. "Having a good time." Alcohol often makes it possible to do things we cannot do while sober. We can feel happy, if we are not happy sober. We can be more forceful if we fear we are not forceful while sober. We can speak our mind, etc. "What's so bad about that?" In such cases a person comes to feel he really needs alcohol in order to live successfully. It becomes an integral part of his way of living. How can a person avoid getting into this situation?

_____

_____

_____

_____

_____

_____

_____

_____

14.   "But I am a great man," I said. "I'm the man who discovered shriveled grapes. I have given the world happiness. You do not appreciate my worth." Because the alcoholic has done great damage to his life and loved-ones, he tends to compensate by imagining himself to be a virtuous person who just happens to drink. This person develops a type of paranoia where he blames others for trying to harm him. What kinds of delusions have you found yourself engaged in?

_____

_____

_____

_____

_____

Notes:

Talking Points for a Group Leader

1. What was this man's unspoken final thought? Can you finish his sentence? What do you think he was about to say? Here are some possibilities. You decide. Circle your answer/s

"I want to tell them that my life has been........"
 a wonderful experience.
 a waste.
 a life of accomplishment.
 lived according to my own principles.
 a rationalization.
 nothing but bad luck.

There is no correct answer. Each individual's answer indicates where they are in their relationship with alcohol. In many cases, an individual will give the answer he/she thinks the group leader wants. The story is written in such a way, that the consequences of drinking are there, but enough of the hero's perspective is portrayed that many can sympathize or associate with him. Ask each individual what his/her answer is and ask why he/she chose that answer. Look for answers that will allow you to get a good dialogue going in the group.

2. "Maybe if I have more, I will be even happier." Early in this person's use of alcohol, he discovered that the more he drank, the more drunk he became. This created a desire on his part to drink as much as possible. What was the result of this thought in his relationship with his wife?

Suggestions:
-They disagreed about the importance and value of the discovery. This is called a value conflict. Value conflicts, if they are about important issues, can ruin marriages.
-It made her wonder about his character as a human being, something she had never wondered about before.
-At this point, they had a different outlook on the importance of raising children properly. He thought of alcohol and disregarded the children.
-They each interpreted problems from a very different perspective. For him, the only problem came when he was sober--and that problem was that he was not drunk. For her, the problem was his drinking and his avoidance of his responsibilities. There are many others. Draw them out in discussion.

3. The first hangover. When he had his first hangover, his reaction was to notice when the pain ended and then start thinking about getting drunk. His wife, on the other hand, discovered the losses from this state and resolved to avoid it. What were those losses?

This point continues the discussion from question 2, except it relates to the value of drinking as such. She realizes that life must go on, things must be done. He believes that the only thing that must go on is drinking. What is a hangover? It is pain that results from the expulsion of alcohol or other drugs from the body. The subconscious mind, no longer anesthetized by the drug, attempts to regain its control over the nervous system. The result is pain and guilt. It happens because of the drug. Elicit as much discussion about this as possible. A hangover should be seen as a reason why drinking is dangerous for the mind and body because it has an effect on the mind's ability to recover its control over life.

4. "I intend to get it as often as I can." This is his decision after discovering the alcoholic state. At this point, a factor outside his control

takes over his life. What is that factor?
Suggestions:
-Alcohol
-Drunkenness
-Avoidance of life's requirements

5. "But it was only an accident and could have happened to anyone. I'll take my chances. It probably won't happen again." Taking chances on walking home drunk (or driving home today) is common among people who drink. Why is this a bad idea?

This discussion is designed to point out, that even if a person drinks, because his judgment is impaired, he may still make a bad judgment to drink and drive. But the choice of drinking and driving can have negative consequences. And "taking a chance" actually makes the individual into a criminal who has violated the law. He is a criminal and this must be stressed. Oftentimes, an individual will make that choice to be a criminal under the premise that he/she will never be caught. Discuss why this is a crucial mistake.

Points of discussion:
• It is against the law
• It does make one a criminal---no matter what one thinks of oneself or how much one has contributed to the community in other ways.
• Accidents are more likely to happen while the individual is impaired
• There are legal and civil liabilities---jail, probation, possible job loss, legal bills and civil damages---that must be taken care of--- because of taking a chance on drinking and driving.
• Sooner or later something will happen.

6. The first dysfunctional family. List the things that happened in this story that point to the breakdown of normal family relations.

Suggestions:
-Value conflicts between man and wife
-Emotional disagreements
-Violence
-Psychologically harmed children
-Physical injury
-Possible legal and financial troubles

7. Herb was the World's first drinking buddy. When two people drink large amounts of alcohol together, what can happen to their friendship?

Suggestions:
-Uncontrollable disagreements
-Fights
-Loud conversation
-Blaming the world for each other's problems (rationalization)

8. Moral choices: "I'll do what I want." This idea puts a person at odds with the responsibilities he/she has chosen and with the people to whom he/she has made commitments. What rationalizations (false justifications) would one have to think in order to allow him/herself to "do what I want?"

Suggestions:
-It's my life
-No one can tell me what to do
-We are responsible for ourselves
-The world is full of do-gooders who want to tell others how to live

Discuss how a rationalization is only an excuse designed to avoid our involvement in a problem, a way of deflecting blame that most often is our own. Point out that a rationalization most often sounds reasonable. But it's purpose is to justify unreasonable actions.

9. Doing things before you can stop yourself. Why couldn't this man control himself while he was drinking heavily?

Suggestions:
-Alcohol intensifies emotions but reduces the ability to make sound judgments
-Alcohol impairs judgment so that when one decides to take action, one is not able to decide if the act is correct

10. "...you blame her for this situation that is your fault." When a person must confront the problems drinking has caused, an easy thing to do is make up a "believable" rationalization. What were some of this man's rationalizations?

Suggestions:

-She didn't drink with me. That was her mistake.
-She threw the pan at me
-She deserted me
-She is cruel

11. Nature's most important law. "You must understand that your mind is your most needed faculty." Why is this so? List examples and reasons why this is so.

Suggestions:
-Our mind makes important decisions
-We need a clear mind to decide correctly
-Our mind is our organ for thinking
-Clear thinking requires an unimpaired mind

12. How does excessive alcohol use violate "Nature's most important law?" List examples below.

Suggestions:
-Lowers reflex responses in our muscular system--this affects judgmcnt
-Does damage to the brain and the entire body
-Thinking patterns used to rationalize behavior are used in other areas of one's life

causing negative results in those areas

13. "Having a good time." Alcohol often makes it possible to do things we cannot do while sober. We can feel happy, if we are not happy sober. We can be more forceful if we fear we are not forceful enough while sober. We can speak our mind, etc. "What's so bad about that?" In such cases a person comes to feel he really needs alcohol in order to live successfully. It becomes an integral part of his way of living. How can a person avoid getting into this situation?

Suggestions:
-Get counseling
-Have non-drinking friends and support
-Take courses in areas where self-confidence suffers
-Confront the problem without aid from mind-altering substances
-Recognize the importance of dealing with issues and having psychological freedom without artificial substances
-Develop a value and goal-oriented approach to life that requires positive action rather than escape

-Learn to think about how you rationalize your behavior

-Recognize that you are either in control of your life or your life is out of control through your own choices--make the choice to control your life without any mind-altering substances

14. "But I am a great man," I said. "I'm the man who discovered shriveled grapes. I have given the world happiness. You do not appreciate my worth." Because the alcoholic has done great damage to his life and loved-ones, he tends to compensate by imagining himself to be a virtuous person who just happens to drink. This person develops a type of paranoia where he blames others for trying to harm him. What kinds of delusions would such a person think?

Accomplishments, real or imagined, cannot cover the fact that one is doing damage to oneself and others, especially family members when one drinks heavily.

Possible examples:
• They hate me
• They are trying to get me

- My wife doesn't appreciate my value
- My wife is trying to put my children between us
- I am a great man
- I have accomplished great things

Group Leader's notes on open discussion:

Appendix A - Alcoholism and Mythology

"Soma appears as third in the Vedic pantheon. The entire ninth book of the Rig Veda is dedicated to Soma pavamāna — soma "in the process of clarification." Even more than in the case of Agni, it is not easy to separate the ritual reality — the plant and the drink — from the god who bears the same name. The myths are negligible. The most important of them relates the celestial origin of soma. An eagle, "flying up to the sky," hurled itself "with the swiftness of thought and forced the bronze fortress" (RV 8. 100. 8). The bird seized the plant and brought it back to earth. But soma is held to grow in the mountains; only a seeming contradiction is involved, however, for mountaintops belong to the transcendental world; they are already assimilated to the sky. Besides, other texts state that soma springs up "at the navel of the earth, on the mountains" (RV 10. 82. 3), that is, at the "center of the world," where passage between earth and sky becomes possible.

"Soma has no attributes except the usual ones that are conferred on gods: he is clairvoyant, intelligent, wise, victorious, generous, etc. He is proclaimed the friend and protector of the other gods; first and foremost, he is the friend of Indra. He is also called King Soma, doubtless because of his ritual importance. His identification with the moon, which is unknown in the Avesta, is clearly documented only in the post-Vedic period.

"A number of details connected with the squeezing of the plant are described in terms that are at once cosmic and biological; the dull sound produced by the lower millstone is assimilated to thunder, the wool of the filter represents the clouds, the juice is the rain that makes vegetation come up, etc. The squeezing is also identified with sexual union. But all these symbols of biocosmic fertility finally depend on the "mystical" value of Soma.

"The texts emphasize the ceremonies that precede and accompany the purchase of the plant and, above all, the preparation of the drink. From the time of the Rig Veda the soma sacrifice was the most popular, "the soul and center of sacrifice" (Gonda). Whatever plant was used by the Indo-Aryans in the early centuries, it is certain that it was later replaced by other botanical species. Soma/haoma is the Indo-Iranian formula for the drink of "nondeath" (amṛta); presumably it replaced the Indo-European drink madhu, "hydromel."

"All the virtues of soma are bound up with the ecstatic experience brought on by its ingestion. "We have drunk soma," says a famous hymn (RV 8. 48), "we have become immortal; arrived at light, we have found the Gods. What can the impiety or the malice of mortals do to us now, O immortal?" (strophe 3). Soma is implored to lengthen "our time to live"; for it is "the guardian of our body," and "weaknesses, sicknesses, have taken flight" (after the translation by L. Renou). Soma stimulates thought, revives the warrior's courage, increases sexual vigor, cures diseases. Drunk in common by priests and gods, it brings Earth close to the Sky, reinforces and lengthens life, insures fecundity. And in fact the ecstatic experience reveals at once the fullness of life, the sense of a limitless freedom, the possession of almost unsuspected physical and spiritual powers. From this comes the feeling of community with the gods, even of belonging to the divine world, the certainty of "nondeath," that is, in the first place, of a plenitude of life that is indefinitely prolonged. Who is speaking in the famous hymn 10. 119, the god or the ecstatic who had just imbibed the sacred drink? "The five (human) tribes did not seem to me worth even a look—have I not drunk soma?" The personage enumerates his exploits: "I have dominated the sky with my stature, dominated the vast earth…. I shall strike this earth great blows…. I traced one of my wings in the sky, I traced the other here below…. I am great, great, I have propelled myself even up to the clouds—have I not drunk soma?" (after the translation by Renou).

"We will not stop to consider the surrogates and substitutes for the original plant in the cult. It is the role that these somic experiences play in Indian thought that is important. Very probably such experiences were confined to priests and a certain number of sacrificers. But they had considerable repercussions by virtue of the hymns that praised them and especially by virtue of the interpretations the hymns called forth. The revelation of a full and beatific existence, in communion with the gods, continued to haunt Indian spirituality long after the disappearance of the original drink. Hence the attempt was made to attain such an existence by the help of other means: asceticism or orgiastic excesses, meditation, the techniques of Yoga, mystical devotion. As we shall see (§ 79), archaic India knew several types of ecstatics. In addition, the quest for absolute freedom gave rise to a whole series of methods and *philosophoumena* that, in the last analysis, opened out into new perspectives and vistas, unsuspected in the Vedic period. In all these later developments, the god Soma played a not very prominent role; it is the cosmological and sacrificial principle that he signified which ended by preempting the attention of theologians and metaphysicians."[18]

---

[18] History of Religious Ideas, Volume 1: From the Stone Age to the Eleusinian Mysteries Kindle Version, Mircea Eliade, Chapter 70. The god Soma and the drink of "nondeath".

The Ten Commandments of Drinking and Driving

This section is intended as a reminder for those of my readers who are presently working on their lives but have not yet stopped driving impaired.

I don't believe that morality should be based on commandments from a divine authority. However, some people have to be told what to do because they can't seem to understand that it does not make sense to be behind the wheel of a huge, expensive and dangerous automobile while under the influence of a drug or alcohol. So here are the Ten Commandments of Drinking and Driving.

Remember, only criminals drink and drive.

I. If you are at home and you have had one or more drinks, STAY HOME.

II. If you are at a friend's house and you have had one or more drinks, STAY THERE, CALL A CAB OR HAVE SOMEONE DRIVE YOU HOME.

III. If you are planning an evening out with friends, DON'T GO OUT WITHOUT A DESIGNATED DRIVER.

IV. If you are driving a group of people to a place where alcohol will be consumed, YOU ARE THE DESIGNATED DRIVER. Don't drink and drive.

V. If you drive to a place where alcohol is being consumed, YOU CANNOT DRINK or

VI. If you drive to a place and have had one or more drinks, CALL A CAB OR HAVE SOMEONE DRIVE YOU HOME.

VII. If you drink and drive and think you will never get caught YOU WILL GET CAUGHT (and hope you do before you kill someone).

VIII. If you think that the police are jerks for pulling you over and charging you with a DUI, GO TO A COUNSELOR (because your actions are not the fault of the police--and you should go to a counselor anyway).

IX. If you think that taking a chance on driving

while drunk is socially acceptable, YOU ARE A CRIMINAL and your social group is a bunch of criminals.

X. If you think that you will never suffer from taking a chance on driving while drunk, YOU MIGHT AS WELL TELL YOUR FAMILY AND FRIENDS THAT YOU WANT TO LOSE YOUR JOB, YOUR DRIVERS LICENSE, KILL YOURSELF AND KILL SOMEONE ELSE (because sooner or later one or all of those things will happen)

Myths of drinking and driving:

Myth #1. I am too much of a man to let alcohol impair me. Besides only sissies can't handle drink.
Answer: People who do not drink are smarter than you.

Myth #2. The police are just a bunch of jerks that want to stop people from having a good time.
Answer: You will have a "good time" after you have killed someone while drinking and driving.

Myth #3. I drink only to relax.
Answer: You drink to get high. You can't handle life straight.

Myth #4. After a long day's work, I deserve a good drink.
Answer: Why does your life require a foreign substance that changes your mental state? If you have worked hard, your body deserves rest not the abuse that alcohol gives it. Get a massage.

Myth #5. I'll never get caught drinking and driving.
Answer: You are a criminal who violates the law. Like any criminal, you deserve to be in jail because society is better off without you on the street.

Myth #6. I can drive normally when I drink.
Answer: Not true. But that isn't important. You are still a criminal when you drink and drive.

Myth #7. I'm not a criminal if I drink and drive and don't get caught.

Answer: Not true. You are a criminal. Just like any criminal…you think you will never get caught…do you know any criminals who haven't spent time in jail? Do you know any criminals who admit they actually committed a crime? What does that make you?

Myth #8. It's ok to have one or two drinks and drive.
Answer: It's not ok. You are still drinking and driving and could still get arrested — or worse, you could have an accident.

Myth #9. If I drink and drive, I won't have an accident.
Answer: Sooner or later you will have an accident.

Myth #10. Drinking and driving is no big deal. People do it all the time.
Answer: You say that to yourself because you just don't want to stop drinking and you're taking a chance on ruining the rest of your life.
Myth #11. Drinking makes me feel more adult.

Answer: Feeling and being are two different things. Only adults are legally allowed to drink. Adults often act worse than children when they drink.

Note: Just think, if you didn't believe in these myths, you might actually be a respectable citizen. You might even be a non-drinker.

ONLY CRIMINALS DRINK AND DRIVE

www.robertvillegas.com

Books by Mr. Villegas Related to Alcoholism

These book use the materials provided in these books to enable both individual and counselors to utilize these materials.

For Counselors:

The World's First Drunk – With Counselor Talking Points

http://amzn.to/2e1R9Kh

The World's First Drunk – Patient's Version

http://amzn.to/2egu62F

The Secular Ten-Step Program Workbook

This booklet is a pocket-sized book that the individual can use on a daily basis to keep track of his thoughts and ideas as he/she works through the Secular Ten-Step Program. Also available in Kindle format.

http://amzn.to/2d9qO09

Business Books by Robert Villegas

These four books by Robert Villegas comprise some of the business books that he has written. As an executive working for several companies, he was able to develop these methods that will help anyone seeking to excel in the business world. These books are:

How to Be a Great Employee – and a Greater Manager

You cannot be a great manager without first being a great employee. And this is something that requires learning, experience and attitude. The attitude comes from you but the learning and experience you should acquire through diligent study and practice. http://amzn.to/2BqdG2i $3.99 Kindle $8.95 softcover

SWOT Analysis Supercharged

A SWOT Analysis is an objective look at the internal and external elements of your organization that impact your success or lack thereof. If done diligently, you will always have a handle on what you need to do to improve season after season.
http://amzn.to/2BCAWYx $3.99 Kindle $6.95 softcover

The Five-Module Call Center Training System

The Five-Module Call Center Training System is designed to assist the Call Center Team Leader in helping his employees quickly upgrade their skills to an acceptable level. http://amzn.to/2B3Svj1 $3.99 Kindle $5.95 softcover

Website Development Methodology

Effective strategic marketing requires the ability to differentiate the website development organization and its deliverables from those of the competition. http://amzn.to/2DnYMqh $2.99 Kindle $12.95 softcover.

www.robertvillegas.com

Alcoholism and Addiction – the System

These four books comprise a system that can be used by both patients and counselors who are battling Alcoholism and Addiction. Based upon Mr. Villegas's own system developed during his struggle against alcoholism, this system includes:

Alcoholism and Addiction – A Secular Ten-Step Program

This groundbreaking book offers a secular approach to alcoholism unlike that offered by Alcoholics Anonymous. We recommend that every individual going for alcohol and drug-abuse counseling be given a copy of this book which contains the workbook and the two versions of The World's first drunk. http://amzn.to/2md6R9w $3.45 Kindle $11.95 softcover

The Secular Ten-Step Program Workbook

This booklet covers the program developed by Mr. Villegas. It is designed as a workbook with blank spaces for the patient to write his own thoughts as he takes each of the ten steps. Order one copy for each patient in counseling. http://amzn.to/2lrHimS $4.49 Kindle $6.95 softcover

The World's First Drunk – With Counselor Talking Points

This booklet is designed for the counselor as he works with patients during individual or group therapy. It contains helpful tips on discussing the life story of the man who invented alcohol. Order one copy for each patient in counseling. http://amzn.to/2l446Wr $2.99 Kindle $5.95 softcover

The World's First Drunk – Patient Version

This version of the short story contains empty spaces where the patient can answer questions about the life story of the man who invented alcohol. Order one copy for each counselor. http://amzn.to/2ldxBGb $2.99 Kindle $5.95 softcover.

www.robertvillegas.com

www.ingramcontent.com/pod-product-compliance
Lightning Source LLC
Chambersburg PA
CBHW060248290526
45789CB00001B/244